489-89

T5-ACX-991

RC-D

Peoples and Nations of
EUROPE

*A short history of
each country in Europe*

Sheila Fairfield

Gareth Stevens Publishing
Milwaukee

Library of Congress Cataloging-in-Publication Data

Fairfield, Sheila.
 Peoples and nations of Europe.

 (Peoples and nations)
 Includes index.
 Summary: A brief history of each country in Europe, arranged alphabetically from Albania to Yugoslavia.
 1. Europe—History, Local—Juvenile literature.
 [1. Europe—History] I. Wojcicki, Mark.
 II. Title. III. Series.
 D22.F35 1988 940'.03'21 88-42919
 ISBN 1-55532-906-3

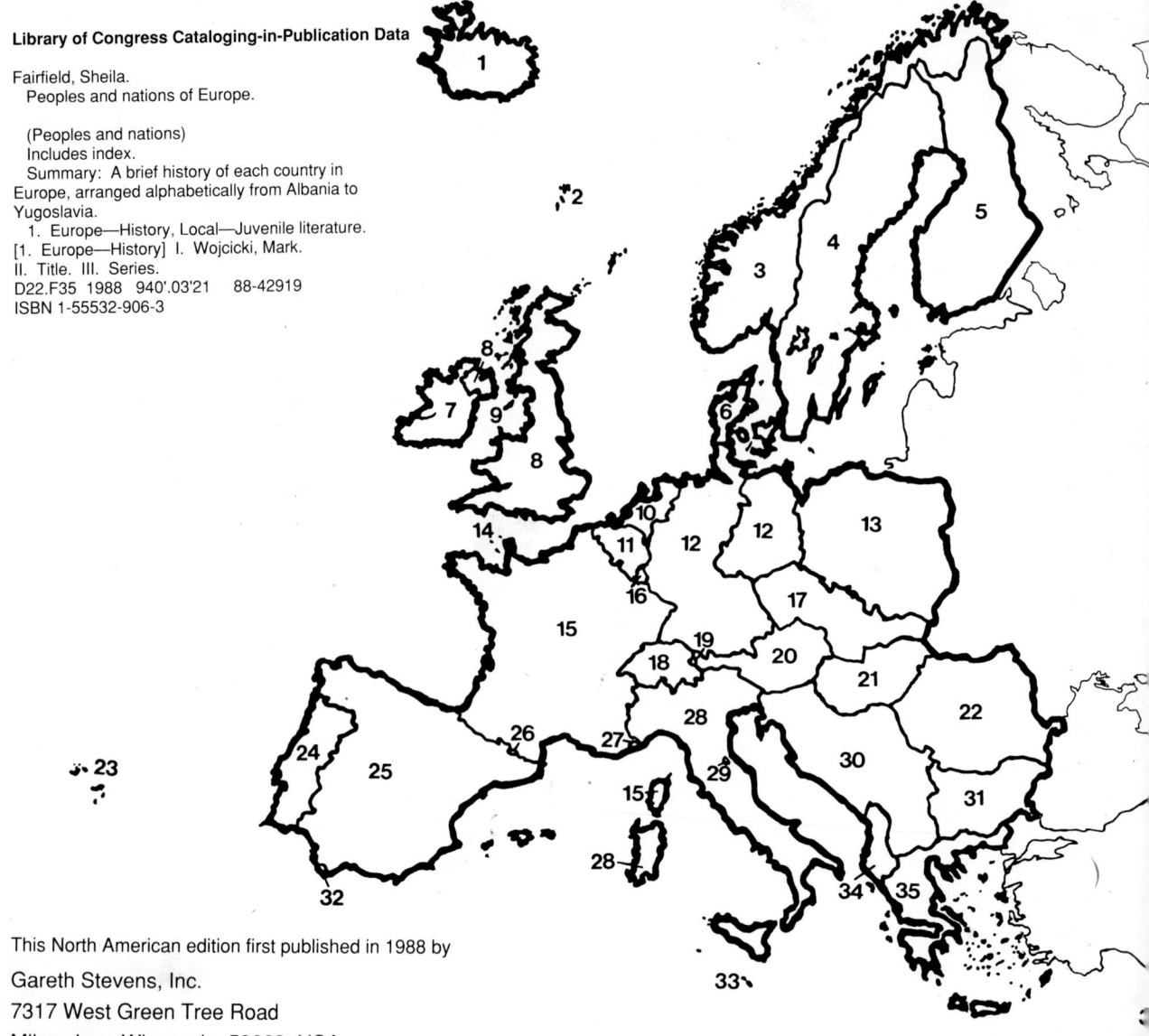

This North American edition first published in 1988 by
Gareth Stevens, Inc.
7317 West Green Tree Road
Milwaukee, Wisconsin 53223, USA

This fully edited US edition copyright © 1988. First published in the United Kingdom with an original text copyright © 1987 by Young Library Ltd.

All rights reserved. No part of this book may be reproduced or used in any form or by any means without permission in writing from Gareth Stevens, Inc.

Designed by Behram Kapadia
Individual country maps by Mark Wojcicki
Full-continent map by Kate Kriege
Picture research by Sara Steel

1 2 3 4 5 6 7 8 9 94 93 92 91 90 89 88

CONTENTS

	Map	Text		Map	Text
Albania	34	58	Spain	25	4
Andorra	26	26	Sweden	4	26
Austria	20	56	Switzerland	18	42
Azores	23	11	United Kingdom	8	44
Belgium	11	6	Yugoslavia	30	24
Bulgaria	31	28	Glossary		62
Channel Islands	14	52	Index		63
Cyprus	36	32			
Czechoslovakia	17	36			
Denmark	6	50			
Faeroe Islands	2	34			
Finland	5	8			
France	15	20			
Germany	12	30			
Gibraltar	32	60			
Greece	35	38			
Holland	10	15			
Hungary	21	53			
Iceland	1	59			
Ireland	7	10			
Isle of Man	9	51			
Italy	28	12			
Liechtenstein	19	9			
Luxembourg	16	23			
Malta	33	49			
Monaco	27	49			
Norway	3	19			
Poland	13	17			
Portugal	24	54			
Romania	22	34			
San Marino	29	60			

A note on the entries in this book: Each nation-state and dependency has a written entry and its own map or a reference to a map elsewhere in the book. Also, some countries include lands that are geographically separated from the main area. These lands do not have a separate entry but are included in the main country's entry. Finally, some countries are mentioned that are part of other continents. They do not have entries here, but you can find them in other volumes of the *Peoples and Nations* series.

SPAIN

Spain is a high, rocky country, cut off from the rest of Europe by the Pyrenees Mountains. There is little fertile soil. Central Spain has bitterly cold winters and hot, dry summers. The most prosperous parts have always been along the east and south coasts by the Mediterranean Sea and along the north coast by the Atlantic Ocean.

Before 1600 BC there were rich cities in the south and east. The people mined precious metal and traded across the Mediterranean. The Phoenicians came from Lebanon to trade before 800 BC. They founded Cadiz. The Greeks came after 600 BC, not only trading but settling. Early Greek farmers brought the first olive trees and the first grapevines. Afterward came the Carthaginians from North Africa. They founded Cartagena.

The Mediterranean coast became a mixture of original Spaniards, Phoenicians, Africans, and Greeks. Inland it was different. Celtic tribes had crossed the mountains from France on to the broad, central plateau. There, and in the north, they lived as shepherds. In the northeast were the Basque people, who sailed, fished, and farmed small plots. They spoke an ancient language unlike that of their neighbors.

In 206 BC the Romans took Spain into their empire. But they did not master the country for two hundred years. There were many uprisings and wars. The fiercest rebels were the Lusitanians, who lived in what is now Portugal. Roman Spain became rich and civilized, but it always depended on tightly controlling the people.

The Roman Empire ended, but the Ro-

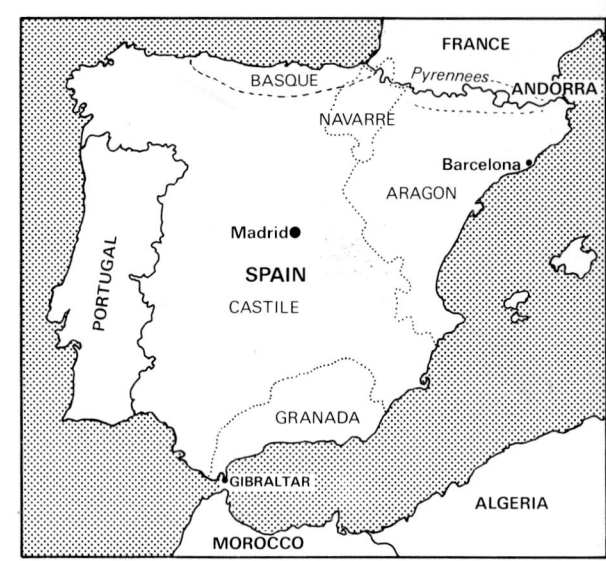

man Catholic Church survived as the central power in Spain. The Church kept the empire's ideas on the need for control.

In AD 711 Muslims from North Africa invaded Spain. They ruled the south. The Catholic rulers they pushed out went north and settled with followers in Asturias.

Under the Muslims, once called Moors, southern Spain had cities, arts, and learning better than any in Europe. Many Spaniards became Muslims, although the Moors did not force them to do so. Southern Spain became a mixture again: Moszarabs, Christian Spaniards living in Moorish areas; Moriscos, Moors converted to Christianity; Mudejars, Muslims living in Christian areas; Moors; and Christians.

There were few people living in the middle of the country. After a time the northerners moved down into the middle, taking more and more of the meager pasture for their herds. Then they built castles to protect themselves; the central land was called Castile, from the Spanish word for "castle." These northerners grew strong enough, in time, to attack the Moors.

By 1248 all Moorish Spain had been conquered except Granada, which remained a kingdom until 1492. There were then several Catholic kingdoms. By 1469 Castile and its neighbor, Aragon, had swallowed all the others, except Navarre in the northeast. In that year, Castile and Aragon were united when their king and queen married. In 1516 Spain was ruled by a Catholic king.

The new country won a great empire, mainly in the Americas, and became powerful in Europe too. Spain was then so important that the Spanish Catholic clergy would not tolerate anyone who disagreed with it.

Then in 1700 a French prince came to the Spanish throne. French kings ruled until 1807. The common people disliked the "frenchified" life of the rich; they began to glorify everything traditionally Spanish. The parts of Spain that were once kingdoms disliked the central rule of the French kings; they kept trying to break away.

During the nineteenth century the link with France ended, and the empire was lost. Arguments broke out. Some people wanted a powerful king and a powerful church. Some wanted a republic and hated the church. Some thought the army should rule. Some wanted a strong central government. Some wanted the old kingdoms to have more freedom. All these arguments at last broke out in a civil war in 1936.

The beautiful Court of Lions is in the Alhambra, the palace built near Cordoba by the Moorish kings who occupied southern Spain for centuries.

After the war, Spain had a republic under General Francisco Franco. It lasted until 1975, when it became a kingdom again. The Catholic Church stopped being the official religion in 1978. Some of the country's regions, especially the Basque country in northeastern Spain, would still like to be independent.

Spain includes the Balearic Islands of Majorca, Minorca, and Ibiza, which lie in the Mediterranean Sea.

BELGIUM

The land now called Belgium used to belong to the Belgae, a fierce tribe of Celts. In 57 BC the Romans defeated them in battle. The Celts and their land were taken into the Roman Empire. The Romans then had to defend the land against other tribes from east of the Rhine. By AD 400 they had allowed one of these tribes, the Franks, to live in their land. They knew that the Franks would keep the others out.

There were then two kinds of Belgians: Celts who had adjusted to a Roman way of life and spoke a language like early French, and Franks who had a northern way of life and spoke a language like Dutch. When the Roman Empire ended, the Franks built an empire in its place.

There were many local rulers, each in charge of a small state, and the emperor was their overlord. By about AD 800 the emperor's rule was weak. Viking pirates raided the country, and the emperor could not fight them off. The local rulers had to do it on their own. When they had succeeded, they wanted more freedom because they knew they could look after themselves.

This lively picture shows a market in Antwerp in the sixteenth century. By this time Antwerp had grown to be the commercial capital of Europe.

On the left you see a lady making lace in the traditional manner. Bruges, in Flanders, has been a leading lace-making town for hundreds of years.

There were also Belgian towns learning to be independent. The Franks had become Christian, so merchants could travel about safely. There were many cargo ships on the Scheldt River and rich trading towns nearby. Ghent, Bruges, Antwerp, and Liege were all important cities.

The Frankish empire split in two in 843. After that the Western Frank kings, who were French, and the Eastern Frank kings, who were German, competed for control of the Low Countries, the area we now call Belgium and Holland. Both found it difficult. The rich towns and small states almost ruled themselves. The most important state was Flanders.

Some time after AD 1000 the population suddenly increased. With less room for farming, Flanders stopped keeping sheep. Instead, it bought wool from England, made it into cloth, and sold it back. People set up small workshops where they made goods for sale. Trade was better than ever, and the people were soon experts in handling money. Many became bankers.

Still, on either side of them were the French and German rulers. Both wanted to be able to tax these rich people. Each ruler also felt that he would be safer if the Low Countries, which were flat and easy to invade, belonged to him.

The Germans — the Hapsburg family — became overlords in 1482. They ruled Austria and many German states. In 1516 they also became kings of Spain.

In 1598 the northern part of the Low Countries rebelled against the Hapsburgs. As a result the area became Holland, an independent country. The southern part did not fight as hard against the emperor, so he was able to keep it. This was mainly because the people, unlike the people of Holland, still shared the Hapsburgs' Catholic religion.

After that there were invasions whenever there was trouble among the Hapsburgs, the French, and the Dutch. The Dutch took the land around the mouth of the Scheldt River. They then stopped Belgian ships from using it.

In 1815 the Hapsburgs and the French lost power in Belgium. The country united with Holland under a Dutch king. The Belgians hated the new rule. In 1830 they rebelled, and between 1831 and 1839 Belgium was accepted as a new country.

The people have been invaded twice since 1900, but they have kept their industries and their prosperity. Belgium is still crowded, with two groups of people and two languages. The Flemish speak a kind of Dutch and the Walloons in the south speak French.

FINLAND

Finland is a low-lying country of forests and lakes. Its few big towns are all in the south. In the north are the Lapps, people who keep herds of reindeer.

The Finns themselves are thought to have come from around the Volga River, in what is now Russia. Finland has a long frontier with Russia, so relations with Russia are important. Finland also has a long coast on the Baltic Sea, across from its other important neighbor, Sweden.

Finland is cold with long winters. There

has never been much fertile land. The early Finns lived on small farms where they worked hard to stay alive. They became tough, but even so there were times when many died of hunger. Young men left Finland to work as mercenaries, hired soldiers in foreign armies.

The Swedes conquered Finland in the fourteenth century. In many ways the country did well under Swedish rule. Farming improved and timber and a kind of tar from the forests were exported. At the same time Swedes brought their language and customs into Finland. The Finns accepted this as long as the Swedes protected them from Russian invasion.

There were many wars between Sweden and Russia, and the Finns were in the middle. Russia conquered Finland in 1808 and held it until World War I (1914-18).

In 1917 there was a revolution in Russia. The new communist government agreed that Finland should be independent. Then, after a civil war in Finland, Finnish communists saw their chance for a revolution in Finland. The communists, however, were defeated with German help.

In 1939 there was a dispute with Russia and a Russian invasion. Then Finland, with Germany, was involved in World War II. When the war ended, Finland had new frontiers: land in the north and east went to Russia, and Finland became the shape it is today. Finns, Lapps, Swedes, and Russians live in modern Finland. Finnish and Swedish are both official languages.

LIECHTENSTEIN

The people of Liechtenstein speak German and are descended from German ancestors. In the Middle Ages, when Germany was made up of many small states, there was a tiny state called Vaduz, which belonged to Count Hartmann III. By 1434 it had reached its present size, only about 62 square miles (160 sq km). Unlike other German states, Vaduz did not become part of modern Germany. Instead it became the Principality of Liechtenstein, which it remains today. The town of Vaduz is the capital. (See map of Germany.)

Most of the country is composed of forests, lakes, and islands, requiring numerous bridges and causeways.

IRELAND

Ireland is an island divided into two states. Most of it is the Republic of Ireland, or Eire as it is called in Irish. The northeastern corner is Northern Ireland, which is part of the United Kingdom.

Celtic tribes arrived in Ireland before 300 BC. Small kingdoms developed under one High King who ruled at Tara. The Irish Celts became Christian after AD 400; Irish monasteries then became important, but the Christian faith did not last everywhere.

After 800 there were raids by Danish and Norwegian pirates, called Vikings. The Vikings were traders as well as raiders. They founded Dublin and other Irish towns as trading stations.

By 1100 there were four kingdoms — Ulster, Munster, Leinster, and Connacht. There was no longer a strong king with overall power. The people lived in tribes or clans, each with its own chief. The tribes had frequent fights with Vikings and raided British coasts for slaves.

The English king wanted to invade Ireland and bring it under his own control. He got his chance in 1169. Dermot, King of Leinster, asked the English king for help against an enemy. English knights were sent to Ireland, but they used Dermot's war as a way to win Leinster and Munster for the English king.

For centuries, the main diet of the Irish poor was potatoes. When harvests failed in the 1840s, there was famine and a huge migration to the Americas.

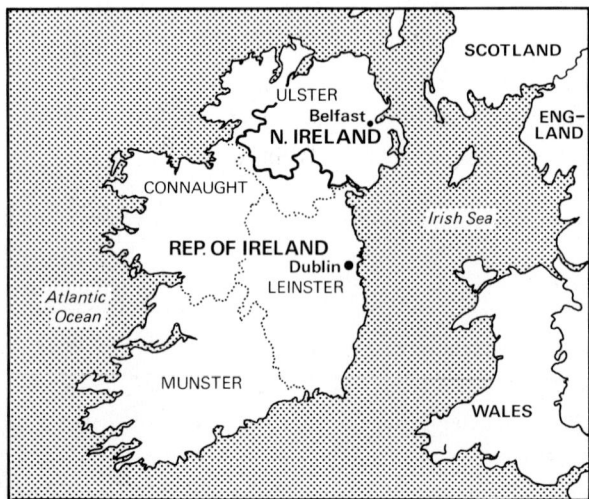

The English were not strong enough either to conquer all of Ireland or to drive the English out. As a result, two different nations began trying to share the island. English lands were held by warlords who were as savage as the Celts, and there were frequent wars.

In the sixteenth century the English conquered the rest of Ireland. They began to impose English law, language, and religion on the people. England was by now Protestant. Ireland had a mixture of Catholic Christianity and older Celtic beliefs, so this conquest was resented as much by the warlords as by the Irish.

Rebellions were stopped. English and Scottish settlers came to farm the land and to live by English law and the Protestant religion. New laws made things easy for Protestants and difficult for non-Protestants.

By the eighteenth century the powerful people were Protestants of Scottish and English descent. Catholics were peasants and so poor they lived on potatoes.

There were more rebellions, and these did bring changes. Anti-Catholic laws were altered in 1829. But in 1845 a disease began to kill potato plants. Famine began in southern Ireland.

Many people died. Others left Ireland for England and the Americas. Most of those who stayed believed English rule did not work and that it should end. But ideas for Ireland's future varied greatly, causing bitter arguments.

Most of Ireland became independent in 1921 as the Irish Free State, later called the Republic of Ireland. Fighting continued because some Irish wanted to keep a link with England and some did not.

Ireland's support of the Catholic James II led to its defeat by William III at the Battle of the Boyne.

Northern Ireland did not join the new state. The people had escaped the famine and were fairly prosperous. They were mainly British and chose self-government within the United Kingdom. Irish Catholics living in Northern Ireland resented this. Arguments turned into riots in 1969, and violence in Northern Ireland has persisted.

AZORES

The Azores is a group of islands in the Northern Atlantic, west of Portugal. They were found by sailors from Portugal, and Portuguese settlers followed. The islands have belonged to Portugal since 1840.

ITALY

Italy stretches from the Alps and down into the Mediterranean Sea. It includes the islands of Sicily and Sardinia. Most of the country is a peninsula, with the Apennine Mountains running down the middle. The good land is in the valley of the Po River, in the north, and in small areas around the coast. South Italy is particularly rocky, dry, and difficult to farm. The north has been richer and is now the industrial part.

From about 800 BC the people of the north were the Etruscans. No one is sure where they came from, and no one has yet translated their language. They lived in cities from which they traded across the Mediterranean Sea.

Farther south, on the plain of Latium, lived the Latin people who first spoke the Latin language. Also to the south was the city of Rome, founded in 735 BC by Latin-speaking people. Farther inland were the Samnites, who lived in the mountains. In the far south and in Sicily lived colonies of settlers from Greece.

After about 400 BC the people of Rome became more powerful than their neighbors. By 275 BC they had control of all other Italian people. Roman government and the Latin language spread everywhere.

Romans were clever, practical, and well-organized. They had a well-trained army and a good civil service. Roman Italy had many cities, rich farms, and all sorts of trade. The Romans built an empire that spread all around the Mediterranean, across Europe to the Rhine and Danube rivers, and across the English Channel into Britain. In AD 395 this enormous empire was halved between two

An artist shows Marco Polo leaving Venice in 1271 for his journey of discovery through Asia. At that time Venice was the busiest port in the world.

The fourth-century Roman emperor Constantine was converted to Christianity. The medieval painting on the right shows him being baptized.

rulers. Rome became the capital of the western half.

There had never been enough Roman — or even Italian — soldiers to keep the huge empire under control. The emperors had gotten used to using warriors from all over Europe. These people were either subjects of the emperor or men from warlike tribes outside the empire who were mercenaries. Some "Roman" soldiers who fought in Britain were actually Germans.

As the western emperors grew too weak to control them, these armies began to fight each other. Then other fierce tribes looking for riches came to join in.

The most important of these last tribes was the Goths. By 493 the empire had come to an end, and Italy was a kingdom. But one important thing had survived from the Roman Empire — the Roman Catholic Church. Its leader was the bishop of Rome, and people even began to think of him as a replacement for the emperors. The Roman Church subdued many of the Goths by converting them to Christianity. But the next invaders were even fiercer than the Goths. These were the Lombards, who invaded northern Italy and then tried to conquer Rome.

The bishop of Rome at that time was Gregory I (c. 540-604). He was already a great religious leader, but now he had to be a commander as well. He fought off the

Lombard invaders with his own armies.

After that the bishops of Rome, later called Popes, were military rulers as well as bishops. They raised armies and fortified towns. As invasions continued, other Italians did the same. Walled cities grew up, especially in the north. These cities had their own governments and controlled the land around them.

During the Middle Ages the city-states were important. They had money, grand buildings, and rich trade. They produced great art. But the cities were rivals and often at war. The greatest cities of the north were Milan, Venice, Genoa, Pisa, and Florence.

Southern Italy had a different kind of state. Normans from northern France had conquered Sicily and the south by 1072. The Normans ruled Sicilians who took many of their ideas and customs from the Greeks and the Arabs.

By 1490, Italy was made up of many of these small states. France invaded northern Italy in 1494. Then, for over 300 years, France, Spain, and Austria fought for power over Italy. The state of Venice, with its trading empire in the eastern Mediterranean, stayed free until 1797. Most of the rest of Italy was controlled by foreign rulers until the 1840s.

By 1848 a movement developed to free and unite Italy. The leader of the movement was prime minister Camillo Benso di Cavour. He was head of one Italian kingdom, Piedmont-Sardinia, and later became king of Italy. In 1861 Italy became an independent country. All but two of the states had joined by 1870. Vatican City, the headquarters of the Roman Catholic Church, remains a separate state ruled by the Pope. The City occupies about 108 acres of the City of Rome. The other state that remained independent was San Marino.

The kingdom lasted until 1946, when Italy became a republic. Although it is a united country, it is made up of a variety of peoples with regional loyalties.

HOLLAND, also called THE NETHERLANDS

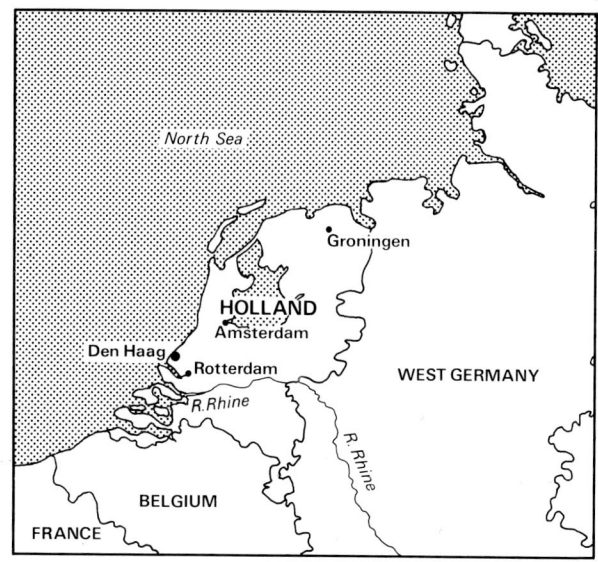

Before 1500 Holland had much the same history as Belgium, but there were two major differences.

Holland was never part of the Roman Empire. Tribes from northern Germany, called Frisians, lived there. The Franks, also from Germany, made Holland part of their empire after AD 800. The Franks and the Frisians had similar customs and spoke the same Germanic language. The people and language of Holland are called Dutch.

Holland had a much longer coastline than Belgium. The Dutch had to spend a lot of time, thought, and money on building walls to stop their flat land from being flooded. There were many small towns and villages along the coast. People lived there in groups to organize the work of protecting the coast.

The Dutch were good at trade. Their big trading cities were near the branches of the Rhine River, which flowed out of Germany, through Holland, and to the sea. Dutch merchants could travel by sea or up the Rhine into the middle of Europe.

After 1500 there was a great reform of the Christian church in Europe. The Dutch took up the new beliefs called Protestantism. They were especially impressed by the leading Protestant reformer and teacher, John Calvin.

The Hapsburgs were the overlords of Holland at that time, ruling it from Spain, which was the center of their empire. The Dutch resented having to pay taxes to a foreign overlord. When the Catholic Hapsburgs tried to stamp out the Dutch people's new Protestant religion, the Dutch rebelled. There was a war that ended in 1598. The Dutch won, and Holland then became an independent country.

The new state was small and crowded, but the Dutch sent out fleets of ships all over the world to trade and found colonies. They also began to make Holland bigger.

Along miles of coast, only the dikes hold back the sea. Here a dike overflows during a storm in 1777.

In the sixteenth and seventeenth centuries the Dutch founded colonies in the East Indies. This painting shows a trading expedition returning to Amsterdam.

They had always been good at keeping the sea out. To make more land they built walls around land that was uncovered at low tide and drained away the water. The walls prevented more water from coming in. This land was very fertile.

Holland's inland frontiers have always been difficult to defend. The country has been invaded many times by the French and the Germans. Germany occupied Holland from 1940-45. Since then, the Dutch have been taking in new people from their old colonies in the East and West Indies. Holland is still crowded, so the Dutch are still working to reclaim land from the sea.

Wool was an important industry in the Middle Ages. This ancient manuscript illustration shows a woman combing out the fibers of a fleece.

POLAND

Before AD 900 a tribe called the Polians used to live in the middle of Poland, around Poznan and Gniezno. They conquered the Masovian tribe who lived to the east, near what is now Warsaw.

The land that the Polians then ruled is the only place that has almost always been Polish. We have to say "almost always" because there was a gap from 1793 to 1807 when it wasn't. Around this piece of land, the shape of Poland has changed over time.

The Polians conquered the Silesians who lived southwest of them. Polians also took control of the country around Kraków in the southeast.

There was a narrow belt of land between Poland and Germany. Slavic tribes lived there who were still pagan, or without a religion, like the Polians. German warlords used to invade the Slav lands. The

warlords often claimed to be good Catholics who were only fighting to stamp out paganism. In AD 963 one of these warlords fought his way right across the belt of Slavic land and attacked Poland.

The Polian chief at once made a pact with the German emperor. The emperor would then stop attacking the Polians, who would then be the emperor's allies. The Polian chief, Mieszko, also said that he would become a Christian and convert his people. In exchange for this, he got the Emperor's protection and took away the Germans' main excuse for attack.

Mieszko also made a pact with the Pope in Rome, who at that time was like a powerful prince. The Pope put the new Catholic Church in Poland under the rule of his own Church of St. Peter in Rome.

Mieszko became Christian to make Poland safe, but in time the Poles became genuine Catholics.

Now that they were allies and had the same religion, the Germans began to influence the Poles. The Poles learned a lot from the Germans, but they also began to worry that the Germans were taking over their country. The pact did not last, and there were fights over ownership of land. Both countries wanted the Slav land that lay between them and, most of all, the land to the north of Poland along the Baltic Sea.

The Poles' eastern neighbors were the states of early Russia. These states were often attacked by hordes of Mongols and Tartars from the east. In 1241 the hordes got through to the frontier of Poland, and the Poles had to fight them off. The Poles won, but the war made them realize the danger of these tribes from Russia. After that, they took some Russian land under their own control whenever they could.

Lithuania, a country northeast of Poland, also won a huge area of Russian land. In 1386 the Queen of Poland was married to the Duke of Lithuania, Jagiello. The two countries formed a union with land all the way from the Baltic coast to the Black Sea. Poland became a powerful country, and it remained so until the Jagiello royal family died out in 1572.

Poland's neighbors remained powerful. There was a new, strong Russian state, ruled from Moscow. There was an Austrian empire to the southwest. Foreign princes were elected as kings of Poland. The princes dragged Poland into their disputes.

In 1772 Austria, Russia, and Prussia, a new state in northern Germany, all took sections of Poland. In 1793 Russia and Prussia took more. In 1795 all three countries took so much more that there was no Poland left. In 1809 the French emperor Napoleon drove out these invaders of central Poland, but he was defeated and his little Polish state came to an end.

In 1815 Poland became a country again, but it was much smaller and had the Russian ruler as its king. For one hundred years the Russians tried to make the Poles become Russian, with Russian language, education, and government. The other parts of the old Poland were either Prussian or Austrian, where the people spoke German.

In 1918 Poland was recognized as an independent country with new frontiers. For the first time since 1772 the Poles didn't need to use all their energy trying to get rid of a foreign government. Now they could build new towns and ports and set up industries in their country. But independence lasted only until 1939.

In 1939 Poland was invaded by Germany from the west and by Russia from the east, at the beginning of World War II. The war ended in 1945, and Poland's borders changed again. Some German land was added to Poland in the west, forcing out the Germans who lived there. Some Polish land was added to Russia in the east, forcing out the Poles who lived there. At the same time, Russia took control of Poland's government, and the country became a communist state.

Poland now has a western boundary roughly where it was in AD 1000. The eastern frontier is a new one, but its middle section is roughly the same as it was after the Russians had had their share in 1795.

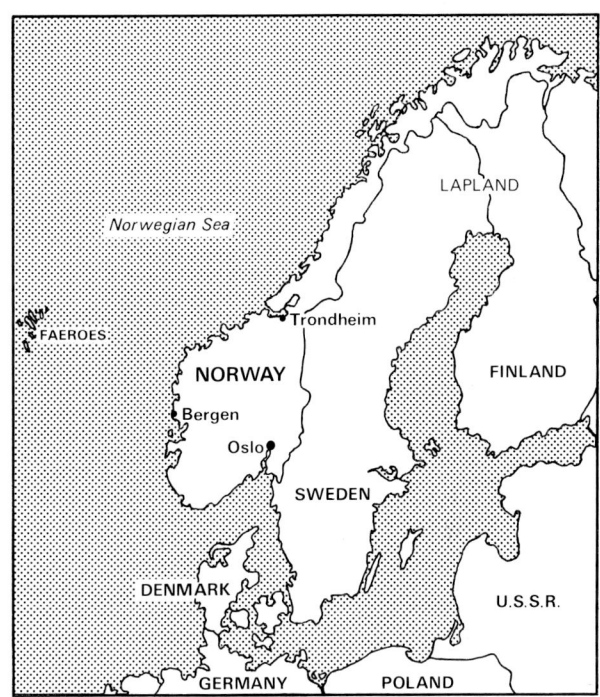

NORWAY

Norway is a long, narrow country with a very long coast. The coast has hundreds of inlets, called fjords, cutting into a mountain landscape. In the far north it is dark day and night during the winter. Most of the people of the north are Lapps. They live by keeping herds of reindeer.

Early Norwegians never had enough good land. Local chieftains traveled with their people, looking for a place to settle. Because Norway was mountainous it was easier to travel by boat up the coast and to settle in the sheltered fjords.

Norwegian people are called Scandinavians. At first all Scandinavians, the people of Denmark, Sweden, and Norway (except the Lapps) had the same language, customs, and religion. After about AD 800 they all sent out bands of warriors by sea, looking for plunder. Other Europeans called these raiders Vikings, whether they came from Norway, Sweden, or Denmark. Vikings also founded colonies and started trade.

Norwegian Vikings settled in Iceland in the Northern Atlantic, and the Faeroe Islands north of the British Isles. Both of these places became colonies of Norway.

This scene depicts Vikings from Scandinavia who were great sea raiders and settlers in the ninth and tenth centuries.

The Arctic island of Spitsbergen became Norwegian in 1920.

The Viking chiefs not only raided other countries but also attacked each other. Norway was not united under one king until 1015. This king was a Christian, St. Olaf. After he was king, Norway was slowly converted to Christianity. Norwegians also began to feel like a separate nation.

There were still civil wars. It was usually the kings of Denmark who intervened when there was trouble. In 1537 Denmark took over Norway, Iceland, and the Faeroe Islands completely. The new Protestant form of Christianity came to Norway from Denmark, as well.

The Danes held Norway until 1814. Then the Norwegians hoped for independence but were joined to Sweden as two kingdoms under one Swedish king. They became impatient with this, and in 1905 they gained independence with a king of their own.

Norwegians still depend on the sea. They have important merchant and fishing fleets as well as energy generated from their mountain rivers. This makes life easier in the north.

FRANCE

The people who lived in France in about 100 BC were called Gauls. They were a Celtic tribe from northern Europe. The Romans made France a part of their empire. They conquered the south first, but it was about sixty years before they controlled all of it because the center of France is mountainous and the Gauls of the north were fierce fighters.

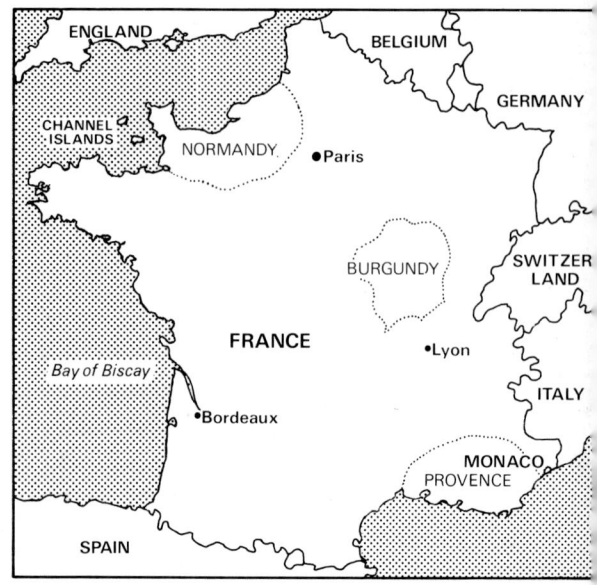

After AD 400 many tribes invaded the Roman empire. One of these, the Franks, won control of France. The Franks were Germans, but they were attracted by the life they found in France. The Gauls, who had become rather like Romans themselves by this time, taught the Franks their language and their Roman ideas. They also took the Franks into their own Roman church.

The Frankish Empire was divided in AD 843, and after that local rulers became more important. The empire had always used the rulers and their armies to defend France. Now local rulers were as powerful as the kings of France. The areas they ruled were like separate countries. The most important were Normandy, Burgundy, and Provence.

Normandy was in the flat north. Normans were Viking raiders from Norway and Denmark who had settled there after AD 900. They were good organizers.

Burgundy was in the east, with big rivers that made travel and trade easy. Burgundians were energetic and full of new ideas.

This illustrates an incident during the Hundred Years' War between France and England. Charles of Anjou is attacked by a British force at Fontenay.

Provence was in the southeast. The people had their own language and many customs and ideas that had come from Italy or Greece. Provence was one of the most "Roman" parts of France.

Other rulers held Brittany, in the far west, as well as Anjou, Aquitaine, and other smaller states.

The king tried to keep his authority over all these places. His great ally was the

Catholic Church. Even after the kings had won absolute power, the Church still had an important place in France, under the king.

After 1500 religion was reformed in Europe, and many people left the Catholic Church to become Protestants. In France this was seen as a threat to the country itself because of the strong Roman Catholic Church there. Civil war resulted.

When the wars were over, the next three kings, ruling from 1610 until 1774, were determined to keep everybody under control.

In all the areas of France, there were the same three groups of people: first, the clergy of the Catholic Church; second, the nobles, some of whom still held large areas of France; and third, everyone else. All these groups had only the rights and the work that the king allowed them. He had total power.

After 1700 the merchants, bankers, and manufacturers became discontented. They had founded colonies overseas and built up trade. They were rich enough to lend the king money. The country's economy depended on them. But rules applied to their group stopped them from rising in society and from taking part in government. They were not even allowed to produce as much in business as they knew they could.

The nobles were also discontented because the king had taken away nearly all their real power. All they had left was authority over the peasants on their own land. They began to enforce their local laws and taxes very severely.

The peasants became very poor. Many even had to leave their homes and beg.

In 1789 the nobles rebelled against the king and ended most of his powers. But without the king they could not control the people. Businessmen saw their chance to get rid of all the old rules that held them back. When the nobles tried to stop them,

the nobles were killed. The poor joined in the killing. Crowds of them caused great destruction. The rebellion became a revolution. France became a republic in 1792. In 1799 one man, Napoleon Bonaparte, took control. He worked out a new code of law and an efficient government for the whole of France. He became emperor.

There were two more periods of royal rule before France became a permanent republic in 1870. By that time France was an industrial country. Most of the people were leaving the country. They went to work in towns near Paris or in the northeast. France today, including the island of Corsica, has about fifty-four million people. Paris and the northeast are still the most crowded areas of France.

LUXEMBOURG

Luxembourg is a small country bordered by Belgium, France, and Germany. It grew up around a fortress, the beginning of the city of Luxembourg. The fortress guarded a road south of the Ardennes Mountains, which was an important military route.

The early people were Celts, like the early French. Luxembourg was part of the Roman Empire until the fifth century, when it became part of the new empire of the Franks, a tribe from Germany. At that time Luxembourg included the present country as well as the southern part of what we now call Belgium.

Shown here is Louis Napoleon, President of the Republic, who was the last Emperor of France from 1852-70.

This area had a series of different overlords. An early count of Luxembourg became emperor of Germany in 1308. The French Duke of Burgundy ruled Luxembourg from 1443 until 1477. Later it passed to the Hapsburg family, whose empire spread from Austria.

During the nineteenth century, Luxembourg was linked with Holland. The country got its present borders in 1839, when part of it passed to Belgium. It became an independent country in 1867.

With such a history, the people speak

French and German as well as their country's language, Letzeburgesch, or Luxemburgisch. Like their Belgian neighbors, most are Roman Catholics.

23

YUGOSLAVIA

The land that is now Yugoslavia used to have two tribes, the Illyrians in the west, and the Thracians in the east. They were there in AD 9 when the Romans turned the whole area into a province of their empire. The Romans called it Illyricum.

In AD 395 the Romans divided their empire in two. The dividing line ran down through Yugoslavia. The north and west were still ruled from Rome and had the Romans' ideas, customs, and language. The south and east were ruled from Istanbul, which was then called Constantinople, or ancient Byzantium. Istanbul was the capital of the eastern, Greek-speaking empire.

In these two empires two kinds of Christian churches developed, the Roman Catholic in the west, and the Greek Orthodox in the east.

The empires were often invaded. During the sixth century a new group of people arrived from eastern Europe. These were the Slavs. In time they took over most of the country and set up seven Slav states.

Slovenia was in the northwest. The Slovene Slavs became Roman Catholics. Their history became linked to that of the powerful Catholic countries next to them — the German empire and, later, the Austrian empire. The country became part German-speaking, part Slovene.

Croatia was in the north. The Croatian Slavs, or Croats, were also converted to the Roman Catholic faith. They learned to write their language in the Roman alphabet. They had many years of rule by the Catholic state of Hungary.

Serbia was in the east. The Serbs, or Serbian Slavs, spoke a version of the Croats' language, which is still called Serbo-Croatian. But they used an eastern alphabet like the one used today in Russia. They learned this alphabet from missionaries of the Orthodox Church who converted them. It was called the Cyrillic alphabet after the missionary St. Cyril. Serbia was an important country. By 1355 Serbian land stretched down into Greece and Albania.

Bosnia-Hercegovina was in the middle. The people never came wholly under eastern or western influence. Many followed the Bogomil religion, not a Christian faith although it included some Christian ideas.

Dalmatia was the coastal strip of land where people lived by shipping, sea trade, and piracy. Hungary, Austria, and the Italian city of Venice all wanted to rule this coast, and Dalmatia was often caught in their disputes.

Macedonia, in the southeast, had many

This shows a Slav army in Hercegovina in 1875 planning an attack on an advancing Turkish military column.

shapes and many overlords. The state became a mixture of Slavs, Bulgarians, Greeks, and Albanians.

Montenegro lay south of Dalmatia, in the mountains. The country was so wild and the people so fierce that no one was able to conquer it until 1945.

All the other states were caught in the great wars between the countries of central Europe and the invading Turks. The Turks were Muslims from Asia who wanted to conquer all of the eastern empire. They first attacked Yugoslavia in the fourteenth century. The armies of Austria and Hungary came to drive them out. When the wars ended, Turkey controlled Macedonia, Serbia, and Bosnia-Hercegovina. Austria or Hungary controlled Slovenia, Croatia, and Dalmatia.

In 1908 Turkish rule ended in Bosnia-Hercegovina, and Austria took control. Many Bogomils had become Muslims under the Turks and rebelled against Catholic Austria. Serbia also encouraged uprisings. Serbians had kept their Orthodox faith and identity under Turkish rule. Serbia had become independent, urging other Slavs to work for freedom. The Turks were driven from all states by 1913. Austro-Hungarian rule ended in 1918.

A new country was then formed, called the Kingdom of the Serbs, Croats, and Slovenes. In 1945 the kingdom became the republic of Yugoslavia, which means "South Slav." There are six Yugoslavian states: Serbia, Bosnia-Hercegovina, Slovenia, Montenegro, Macedonia, and Croatia, including Dalmatia.

ANDORRA

Andorra is a republic lying on the border between France and Spain in the Pyrenees Mountains. The people are of mixed French and Spanish descent, and both languages are spoken. The official language is Catalan, a kind of Spanish. The President of France and the Bishop of Urgel, in Spain, jointly rule Andorra. (See map on page 4.)

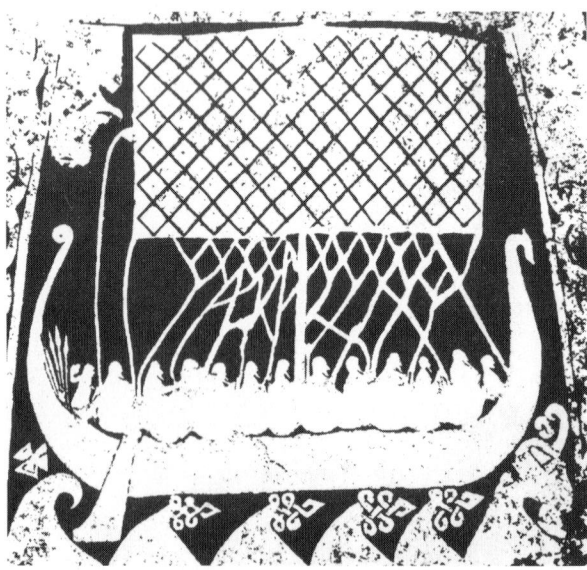

This is a huge slab of stone, decorated in medieval times with a carving of a Viking ship.

SWEDEN

The earliest important Swedish kingdom that we know about was in the region where Stockholm is now. This was the kingdom of the Svear people. The other important areas of the country were not on the mainland of Sweden but on the Baltic Sea islands of Gotland and Öland.

The Romans wrote about the Svear people before AD 400. They said the Svear had a strong fleet of ships, were good at trade, and loved riches.

After about AD 800 a new people from Sweden became widely known. These were the Vikings — a name for the pirates who raided on the Baltic Sea and from the North Sea coasts of Norway and Denmark. Vikings from Sweden went eastward up the Baltic, along the coast of Finland, and into the mouths of Russian rivers. They sailed far into Russia and found the great trade routes into eastern Asia. They became merchants as well as pirates. Once again, Sweden became rich through trade.

However, the country was still quite small. What is now the southern tip of Sweden was then part of Denmark, and the

north had hardly been explored. Olof Skötkonung was king of Sweden from about the year 1000. He ruled Öland and Gotland, the old Svear lands around Stockholm, and two areas west of Stockholm called Ostergotland and Vastergotland.

Olof was the first Christian king, but the Swedes still believed in the Vikings' gods. They were not converted to Christianity in large numbers until after 1100.

During the fourteenth century, Sweden conquered Finland, enlarging its territory by clearing northern forests. Farmers settled there to work small plots of land. German miners settled in the mountains to mine iron and copper. German merchants set up towns where they bought the metal for export.

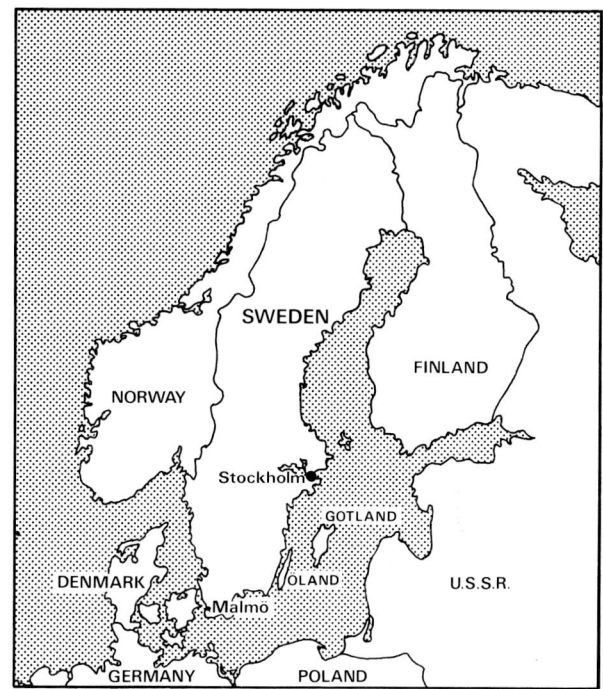

It was through Germans that the Protestant religion came to Sweden in the sixteenth century. The new beliefs, taught by the German reformer Martin Luther, were established in Sweden by 1550.

When the German Protestant states were attacked by the German emperor, the Swedish king Gustavus Adolphus (1611-32) led his armies into Germany to defend them. Sweden became very important during these religious wars and also became the friend of many German states.

Sweden fought wars with Denmark. Both countries wanted to be the strongest in the area around the Baltic Sea. In 1660 the Swedes conquered the fertile Danish land in what is now southern Sweden.

The Battle of Lutzen in 1632 shown here was a brilliant victory for the Swedes in the Thirty Years' War. Their leader, Gustavus Adolphus, was one of the great military geniuses of history.

During the next hundred years Russia became more important in northern Europe, and Sweden became less so. Russia drove the Swedes out of Finland in 1808. In 1814 Sweden began a union with Norway that lasted until 1905.

Since then Sweden has had its present borders. The north reaches up into the Arctic, where the winters are dark and bitterly cold. Most of the people live in the south. Like their neighbors in Norway and Denmark, they are called Scandinavian.

BULGARIA

Bulgaria has two big rivers. The Danube flows through low-lying country in the north, the Maritsa through its own valley further south. In between the two, and in the far south, there are mountains.

The Thracians, skilled with horses, were the early people of Bulgaria. They were conquered by the Macedonians under King Philip II (359-336 BC). Many Macedonians were of Thracian descent, and the two peoples mingled easily. However, Macedonia's empire was conquered by the Romans, and in 46 BC Bulgaria became part of the Roman Empire.

In AD 395 the empire was divided in two. Bulgaria was part of the eastern half. The eastern emperor ruled from Byzantium, which is now Istanbul. Greek was the language of the eastern empire. When Christianity spread, it did so as the Greek Orthodox Church grew.

The emperors were seldom strong enough to keep out enemies. Bulgaria was on the edge of the empire, and it was

In the Eastern Orthodox Church, an icon is a sacred picture. This one in a thirteenth-century church depicts St. George the Crowned.

28

invaded by two powerful tribes. The Slavs came from eastern Europe in the sixth century. Slavic language and ways of life spread through the country. Then, in the seventh century, the Bulgars came. They did not conquer the Slavs as the Slavs had conquered the original people. Instead they learned the Slavs' language and copied their customs. Both tribes in time became Eastern Orthodox Christians.

The Bulgars fit into the eastern empire quite well, but their leaders would not always agree to be ruled by the emperor. Sometimes they broke away altogether.

During the ninth and tenth centuries they conquered more land and set up an empire of their own, but the emperor brought them back under his control in 1018.

The Turks, who were Muslims, invaded the empire from Asia. They defeated the Bulgars in 1371 and had control of Bulgaria before 1400.

The Turks allowed the Bulgarian language and the Greek Orthodox Church to survive. But during the nineteenth century Turkish rule became very harsh, causing the Bulgarians to want freedom. They got their freedom in 1908, but they also wanted the new, free country to be much bigger. There had been links between Bulgaria and Macedonia since before Roman times. Now

This is the Valley of Roses. Millions of rose bushes are grown here for the manufacture of perfume.

there were many Bulgarians living in Macedonia who wanted their country to be part of the new Bulgaria.

There were wars, and many arguments about the frontiers. Bulgaria's present frontiers were not fixed until 1947.

During World War II, Bulgaria took Germany's side against Russia. Russia invaded Bulgaria in 1944 and set up a government that was friendly to Russia. The present communist People's Republic of Bulgaria was founded in 1946.

GERMANY

There used to be many tribes in Germany. All had different customs, but their language was similar. They spoke the Germanic languages, and the tribes were called Germanic, or German. The most important tribes were the Franks, Saxons, Bavarians, Alemanni, Thuringians, and Frisians. Until about AD 400 their western boundary was the Rhine River.

By AD 804 the Franks had conquered all the tribes. They had also conquered France, and Charlemagne, king of the Franks, ruled France and Germany. His grandsons divided his empire in 843. Germany was then separated from France, and for centuries there were arguments about where the dividing line should be.

Germany had hundreds of states, some big and important, some tiny. Apart from the mountains of the south, Germany had few natural defenses. In 911 the last Frankish king died, and the small states knew they could not fight off their enemies on their own. They chose a new king as a warlord to protect them against Danes in

the north and Slavs and Magyars in the east. The states helped the king with the actual fighting, so for many years it was normal for a German state to be run like an army.

In 962 the German king, Otto I, was made an emperor. He was crowned in Rome, by the Pope, as Holy Roman Emperor. He was supposed to be the Roman Catholic leader of what had once been the Roman Empire in Europe. From then on, German kings became more and more involved with events outside Germany. The state rulers took more power for themselves. They became rivals for power and there were frequent wars.

After 1100 many states had more people than they could feed, so they cut down the forests and drained the marshes to make more farmland. They also moved east onto land that belonged to the Slavs. They had beaten the Slavs in battles before, but this time German soldiers were followed by thousands of German settlers. The land was good for grain because of this and became important in trade.

The rulers of smaller states tried to keep out of the wars. They competed in peaceful pursuits, like commerce and learning. German merchants formed a powerful league, called the Hanseatic League, to build up their trade. The league became strong enough to set up German colonies in many trading cities of northern Europe. State rulers set up universities and encouraged printing. Then educated people all over Germany were able to read and discuss each other's work. People were reminded that they had a language in common. Whichever state they lived in, they were all Germans and they formed a nation.

Opposite: Before the majestic Brandenburg Gate lies the modern wall, built by the East Germans in 1961 to separate the two halves of Berlin.

Before the Diet (parliament) of Worms in 1521, Luther refused to recant, or take back, his teachings against Catholic doctrine.

One of the new German scholars was Martin Luther. In 1517 he set out to reform the Roman Catholic Church. Many German Christians followed him. A new German church broke away from Catholicism and called itself Lutheran. Whole states took up the new faith.

The Emperor, a Catholic ruler, tried to win Lutherans back by force. There were wars until 1648. By then Austria and the rest of southern Germany were still Catholic. Northern Germany was Lutheran; its most important state was Prussia, which was in the northeast.

Prussia lay on the grain-bearing lands that had been taken from the Slavs. A Prussian's main work was to farm the land and support the army in northern Germany.

Prussia became more powerful until, in 1871, the state was able to set up a new united Germany without Prussia's main rival, Austria.

This time, national unity was a fact, not just a feeling. But many states resented Prussian control. After World War I the Prussian king of Germany had to abdicate, and a republic was founded in 1919.

The frontiers were changed by World War I (1914-18) and World War II (1939-45). The main arguments were about the frontiers with other countries: France, Poland, and Czechoslovakia.

United Germany came to an end in 1945, after World War II. Now there are two German states. The Federal Republic in the west includes many of the old states. It still has a Catholic south and a Lutheran north. The Democratic Republic in the east is a communist state. It was formed during the Russian occupation, after 1945, in what used to be Prussia.

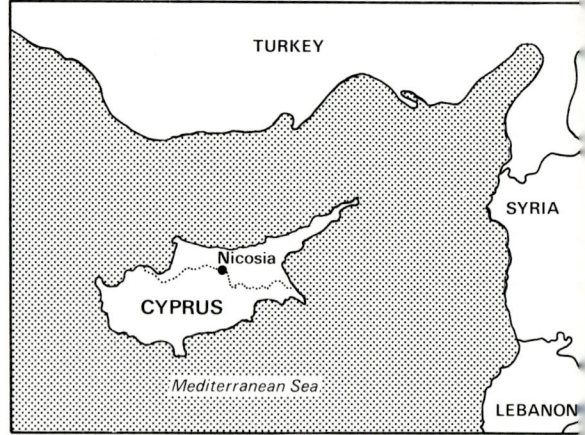

CYPRUS

Cyprus is a small island republic in the eastern Mediterranean sea. Its nearest neighbors are Turkey and Syria, both in Asia.

The earliest invaders that we know about were Greek. They came as traders in about 1400 BC. Later, more Greeks came and settled there. Greek life and the Greek language spread throughout the island.

By AD 60 Cyprus was part of the Roman Empire. At about that time, St. Paul and St. Barnabas visited Cyprus and converted the Roman ruler to Christianity. The Roman empire split in two in AD 395. Cyprus was part of the eastern, Greek-speaking half, so Christianity in Cyprus took the form that was called Greek Orthodox.

The empire came to an end gradually, as the emperors failed to keep their enemies

Here, on Christmas Day, AD 800, the Pope crowns Charlemagne, King of the Franks, as the first Holy Roman Emperor in St. Peter's Church in Rome.

The Roman mosaic on the right shows a scene in Cypriot life. Cyprus became a Roman province in 58 BC.

out. During the twelfth century, armies from western Europe invaded the area. Cyprus was held by western European rulers until 1571, when it was taken by Turkey. The Turks held it until 1914.

During all that time, western invaders had little effect on the original Greek life, customs, and language. The Turks, however, had come from only a few miles away. They found it easy to settle in northern Cyprus in large numbers. By 1914 there were two communities. The Greeks were, and still are, the larger of the two.

Cyprus was British from 1914 until 1959. Since then Greeks have fought for Cyprus to be part of Greece, and many Turks have fought for it to be part of Turkey. In 1933 the Turkish part of the island was declared to an independent state, but the argument continues even today.

FAEROE ISLANDS

The Faeroes is a group of a very small Danish islands that lie to the north of the British Isles. Viking sailors from Norway landed there about AD 800. At that time the only inhabitants were monks, whom the Vikings drove out. The islands were then ruled by Norway until 1537, when they became Danish.

ROMANIA

Romania is the easternmost country on the Danube River. The river flows through the south to a big delta on the coast of the Black Sea. Northern Romania is mountainous.

The early people were Thracians, living as shepherds and moving into defended villages when there was danger. The Romans conquered them and called their land Dacia. The people accepted Roman rule and customs. The Romanian language has much in common with Latin, the Romans' language.

After AD 270 the Romans had to leave Dacia undefended because their empire had grown too big to protect. People moved away from the Danube plain, which was easy to invade. They went to the mountains of Transylvania, and there they lived safe from invasion for centuries.

In 896 the Magyars, a warlike people from the east, conquered Transylvania. The Magyars and, later, the Germans, who were the Magyars' allies, came to live in it. Romanians living in Transylvania had to adjust to two groups of foreign people, two foreign languages, and a western religion — the Roman Catholic Church. Many left the mountains and moved back to the lowlands near the coast.

In the early fourteenth century the Romanians founded two independent states. Walachia was in the south and Moldavia was in the east. There they had their own kind of Christianity, the Eastern Orthodox Church, that had spread through the eastern part of the old Roman empire, to which Romania had belonged.

This old empire was now being attacked by Turks, who were Muslims from Asia. Walachia came under Turkish control in 1393, Moldavia in 1455. By that time Transylvania was not only ruled by Magyars but joined to the Magyar kingdom of Hungary. The Turks conquered it in 1526 and the people — Romanians, Magyars, and Germans — came under Turkish rule.

The Turks did not force people to become Muslims. Many did convert, but the Orthodox church survived in Walachia and Moldavia, and so did the Catholic church in Transylvania. After 1526 Transylvania also

On the opposite page, during an uprising at Braila in 1907, a priest tries to persuade Romanian peasants to go away peacefully.

had two of the new Protestant Christian sects. Many Germans became followers of Martin Luther, while many Magyars became followers of John Calvin. In 1699 Transylvania was recaptured by the new rulers of Hungary, who were Catholics, but by that time the Protestant churches were well established.

Moldavia and Walachia were part of the Turkish empire until 1878. Then they became independent and joined together as the state of Romania. In those days the country's name was spelled "Rumania."

In 1918-19 Transylvania broke away from Hungary and joined Romania. But many Germans and Magyars still live there. Also in 1919, Romania gained some land to the east. This was lost again, to Russia, at the end of World War II in 1945. Romania was important during that war because it had large oil fields valued by countries on both sides.

Modern Romania is a socialist state with a communist government.

CZECHOSLOVAKIA

There are three parts to Czechoslovakia: Bohemia is the western part, Moravia is the middle part, and Slovakia is the eastern part.

In Bohemia and Moravia Germanic people drove out early tribes. The country lay along the edge of the Roman Empire. Germanic tribes came together along this edge. While the empire lasted, it was as far as they could get. They settled in Bohemia and Moravia, but before AD 500 they had been invaded by Slavs from what is now Russia. They moved west through Europe as far as the mountains of Austria and the big rivers of eastern Germany. Different Slavic tribes invaded all three parts of Czechoslovakia. Those who came to Bohemia and Moravia were Czechs. Those who came to Slovakia were Slovaks. They speak separate but similar languages.

During the ninth century Moravia became the center of an empire called Great Moravia. This included Bohemia, Slovakia, present-day Hungary, and parts of what are now Germany and Poland.

The people converted to Christianity. For a long time it was not certain whether they would turn to the Roman Catholic Church or the Eastern Orthodox Church. Most Slavic countries became Orthodox, but missionaries from the neighboring German state of Bavaria converted the Czechs to Roman Catholicism. At about the same time, Slovakia was conquered by the Magyars. These people came from the east but they were not Slavs. Their kingdom was Hungary, so Slovakia was part of Hungary until 1918.

The empire of Great Moravia came to an end. In 1029 Moravia and Bohemia became a new country under one prince. The country was independent, but the prince had an overlord, the German emperor. Bohemia also had many German settlers, especially near the western frontier. The settlers farmed the land, mined metals, and built towns.

When the native rulers died out in 1306, it seemed natural to offer the throne to a German prince.

The second German prince to rule the Czechs became the German emperor as well. He made the country part of a league of Catholic states. The Catholic Church became very rich. The Czechs thought of it as a German church. They resented its wealth and wanted a Czech church where they could worship in their own language.

A Czech priest, Jan Huss, began to reform the church after 1390 and encourage the use of the Czech language in church. His followers turned his campaign into a national revolt. Armies of "Hussites" fought

Prague, the capital city, has many fine old buildings and statues. Here crowds gather in front of the astronomical clock on the wall of the Town Hall.

against armies of the German emperor.

The Hussites, however, could not agree with each other. Hussite landowners were envious of rich Hussite towns and frightened of the peasant armies, so the Czechs could not unite.

In 1526 another German ruler became king of Bohemia and Moravia. He was Ferdinand of Hapsburg, Duke of Austria. Under Hapsburg rule there were more revolts. All revolts had failed by 1620. After that, the country was Roman Catholic and German-speaking.

The Hapsburgs built an enormous empire of German, Magyar, and Slavic peoples. The Czechs lived as part of this empire until 1918. They were well ruled by the Hapsburgs, but many disliked being turned into Austrians, as the Hapsburgs were rulers of Austria and ran their huge, far-flung empire from Austria.

By 1800 all the more intellectual people spoke German while the peasants and the poorer villagers spoke Czech. But social reforms improved the lives of the Czech-speaking people. They turned to fellow Slavs in nearby countries for support and began to work for freedom from Austria.

The Austrian empire broke up when World War I ended in 1918. An independent Czechoslovakia was founded, including Slovakia, Bohemia, and Moravia.

In 1938 the Germans took the parts of Bohemia that had a mainly German population. In 1939 they conquered the rest of the country. The German invaders were driven out in 1945. By that time the Czechs felt strongly anti-German, and they drove out many of their own German-speaking people too.

A communist government then took power. Czechoslovakia became a member of the Slavic group of communist countries in eastern Europe.

GREECE

The mainland of Greece is mountainous, with the Pindus Range running down the middle. Greece also includes many islands in the Aegean Sea and the Ionian Islands in the Adriatic Sea. Modern Greece stretches north and east across fertile farmland. But early Greece was much smaller.

The biggest Greek island is Crete. Here, a people earlier than the Greeks were already rich and civilized before 2000 BC. Crete was a stopping place for seafarers between Europe, Africa, and the Middle East. But the Aegean was a place of earthquakes and volcanoes. The kingdom of Crete ended suddenly. It was probably destroyed when the nearby volcano of Santorini blew up.

The first Greeks came from north of the Aegean Sea and settled all around its shores. They arrived in mainland Greece about 2000 BC. There were two important tribes already there, the people of Attica, whose center was Athens, and the people of Arcadia, whose center was Argos.

The early Greeks became very powerful. Mycenae was the main fortress of great warlords for about 700 years. Then there was another invasion. The Dorians, who also came from the north, spoke a form of Greek. They were less civilized than the Greeks and warlike. Southern Greeks began to come together in fortified cities for defense. In time these cities became the centers of states. The most important cities of ancient Greece were Athens, Sparta, Argos, Corinth, and Thebes.

The people of the city-states produced great art, ideas, and forms of government that have influenced a large part of the world ever since. They founded colonies all around the Aegean coast. Much of modern Turkey was Greek at that time. But they were often at war with each other as they competed for sea power.

North of the Greek states lay Macedonia and Thessaly. There lived Thracians and Illyrians from what are now Bulgaria and Yugoslavia as well as Greeks. Macedonia, under Philip II and Alexander, conquered Thessaly and Greece and made one large Greek empire. This empire was conquered by the Romans in 148 BC.

The Romans admired the Greeks. They copied their art and studied their ideas. When the Roman Empire was divided in AD 395, the eastern emperor set up his capital at Byzantium. This city, later called Constantinople and now Istanbul, had been a Greek colony. It became a center of Greek culture which spread through the eastern empire. In time, eastern Christians broke away from the Christian church of Rome and founded the Greek Orthodox Church.

This eastern empire and its Greek culture lasted until the fifteenth century, but it was not always strong enough to keep out invaders. Slavs from eastern Europe settled in Greece after the year AD 500, learned the Greek language, and became Orthodox Christians. Later on came Albanian settlers and Vlachs from Romania.

Armies from western Europe also attacked the empire, looking for plunder. The Greeks disliked and distrusted the west, especially the Italian states. They

Salonika, with its many mosques, was still a Turkish city when this picture was drawn in 1876.

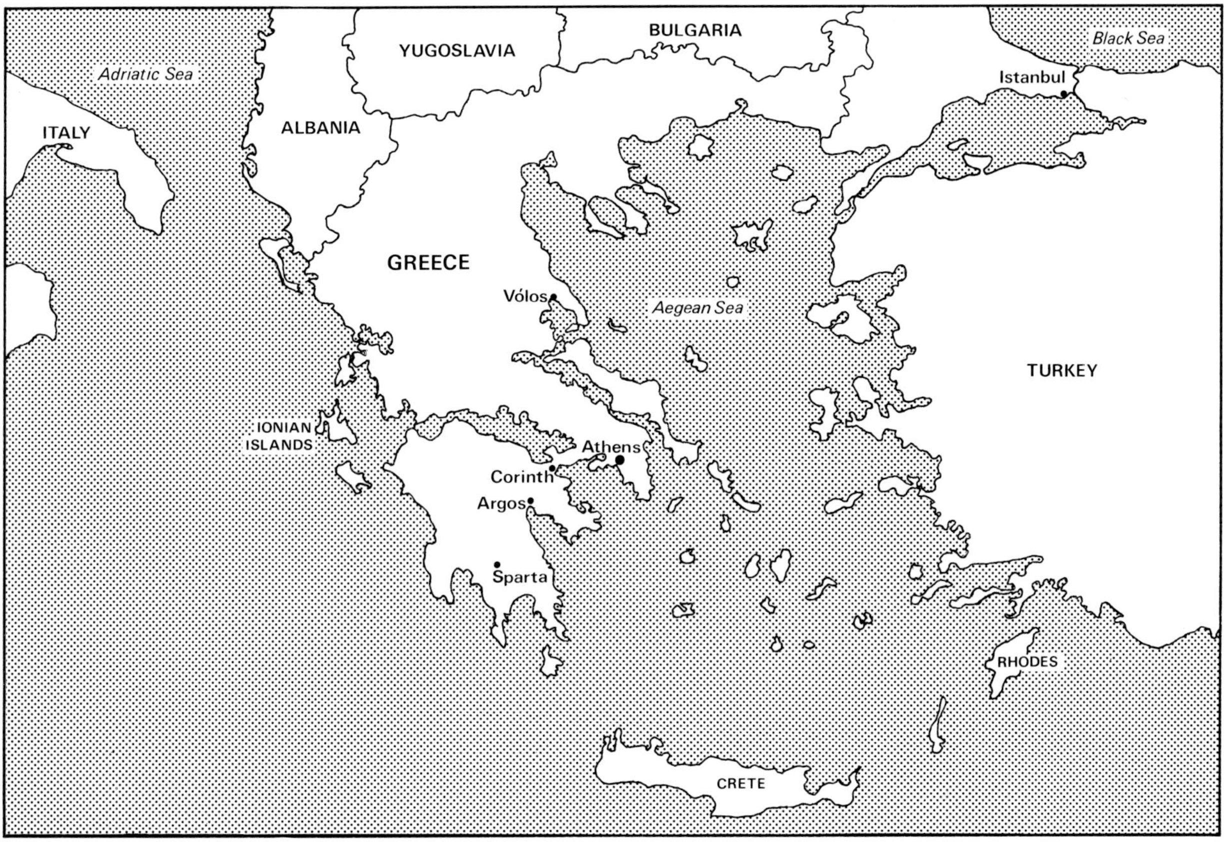

YUGOSLAVIA
BULGARIA
Black Sea
Adriatic Sea
Istanbul
ITALY
ALBANIA
GREECE
Vólos
Aegean Sea
TURKEY
IONIAN ISLANDS
Athens
Corinth
Argos
Sparta
RHODES
CRETE

sometimes felt they had more in common with their eastern neighbors, the Turks. When the Turks invaded from Asia, they were able to win Greece by 1460.

The Turks paid most attention to the fertile land and the cities. They left the mountain people alone. They tolerated the Greek language and the Orthodox Christian faith. Only in the last years of Turkish rule were they cruel oppressors. The Greeks rebelled in 1821 and drove the Turks out by 1832, forming an independent Greece.

The new state was small. It included the mainland as far north as the Gulf of Volos and some of the islands in the Aegean. There was little fertile land. Most of it was held by Turkey.

The Greeks remembered their once great empire. So during the next one hundred years, they slowly recaptured land, until Greece was more than twice as big as it was in 1832. Macedonia is now divided. The name is used for a part of northern Greece and for a part of southern Yugoslavia.

Above, a tiny town on the Aegean island of Siphnos. Right, the amphitheater at Donona, famed since classical times as the site of the oldest Greek oracle.

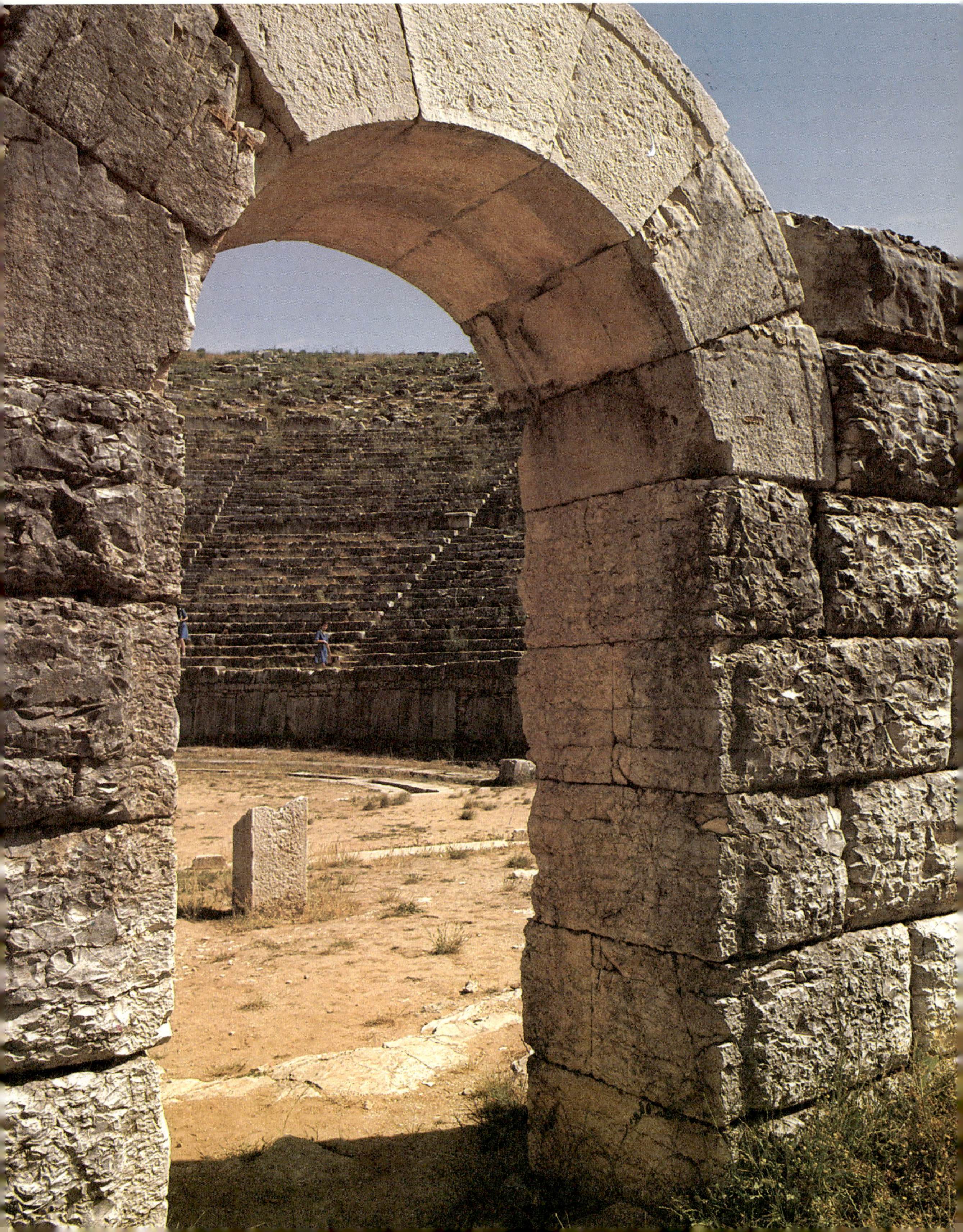

SWITZERLAND

The west and center of Switzerland are made up of high, hilly country that is good for farming and growing vines. Most of the rest is mountainous, with deep river valleys in between.

The Romans invaded Switzerland after 58 BC. The people they conquered were Celts. The Rhine River, which was the Romans' northern frontier, still forms most of the northern boundary of Switzerland.

When the Romans left, tribes from Germany began coming across the Rhine to settle in north and central Switzerland. Other tribes of Burgundians, from part of what is now France settled in the west. Italian tribes moved into the south. In the east "Romanized" Celts were left in control.

Four groups of Swiss remain who speak German, French, Italian, and an old Roman-Celtic language called Romansch.

In the Middle Ages much of Switzerland belonged to a few powerful families. The most powerful were the Hapsburgs. They became rulers of Austria and emperors of all the German states.

Most people in Switzerland lived in communes. These were small groups of people who kept together so they could make the best of their farmland, pasture, woods, and fresh water. When the Hapsburgs became powerful, the communes began to join together to defend their rights and to form leagues.

These leagues were the beginning of the present Swiss states, or cantons. They fought for independence from the German emperor, and they fought off outside enemies from Italy and Savoy, an old state which became part of Italy and, later, part of France. They also disagreed with each other. There was a lot of warfare. By the time they had won independence in 1499, Swiss soldiers were probably the best in Europe. Swiss men often earned a living by fighting in the armies of other countries.

During the sixteenth century the Christian church in Europe was reformed. Switzerland was, and still is, divided between the old Catholic and the newer Protestant religious beliefs.

All the present states became a confederation, or group, in 1848.

Outside the big towns people still live in communes. Each commune has some good land, some pasture, some woodland, and enough water. Each group of people lives together in a river valley, separated from each other by the mountains. Switzerland is a gathering of many small units, all of which like to be as independent as possible.

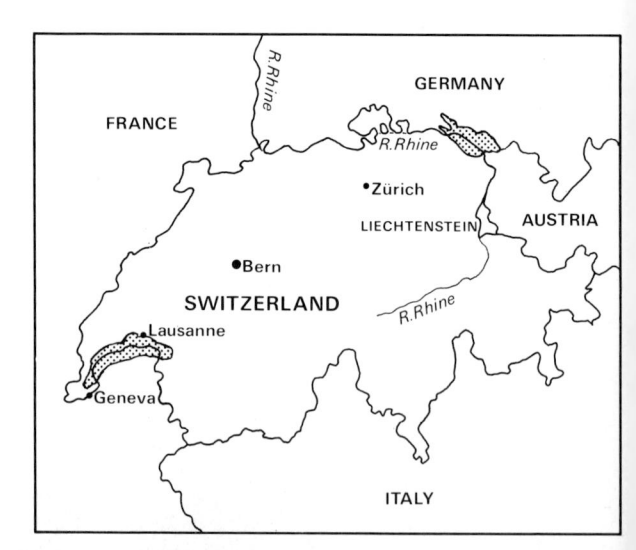

The Swiss have been exporters of cheese for centuries. Here a peasant of the Toggenburg district makes the cheese in a large copper kettle over an open fire.

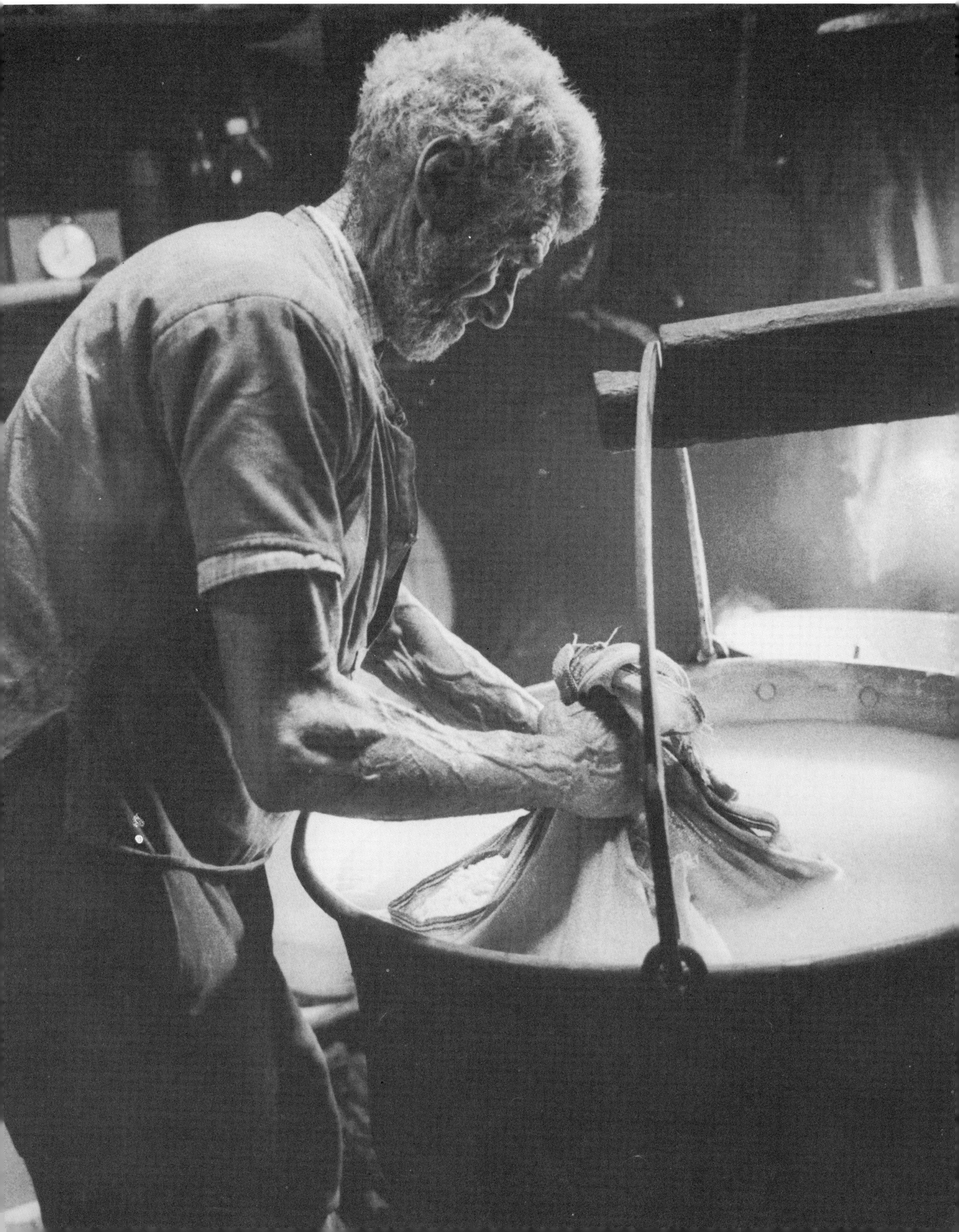

UNITED KINGDOM

The name "United Kingdom" means the United Kingdom of Great Britain and Northern Ireland. Great Britain is the largest island of the British Isles. It is made up of England, Scotland, and Wales.

The Romans visited England in 55 BC. They found Celtic tribes very like the people they had conquered in France. Celts were lively and clever. They were also warlike and used much of their skill in metalwork to make weapons and armor.

The Romans invaded England in AD 43, but conquest took forty years. By then the tribes of England were used to Roman ways of living and Roman law. They took up the Christian religion as it spread through the Roman empire.

The Christian religion also reached Wales, but the Welsh Celts were not much affected by Roman rule in other ways. Their country was mountainous and difficult to conquer.

The same was true for the Scottish Celts, although for a short time the Romans had a northern frontier in what is now central Scotland. All the tribes who lived beyond it were known to the Romans as Picts, or "painted ones," because they decorated themselves with patterns like tattoos. After AD 196 the frontier moved out of Scottish land and south to Hadrian's Wall, which runs between the Solway Firth and the mouth of the Tyne River.

Then the Scottish tribes were independent again, although some were allies of the Romans against the Picts. Other Celts came from Ireland to settle in Scotland, mainly in the south and west.

Roman rule in England ended after AD 400. The English Celts had no unity, so after 450, when more invaders came, the Celts could not band together to keep them out. These invaders were from northwest Germany and parts of Denmark. They were Angles, who settled in eastern England and Scotland, Jutes who settled in Kent, and Saxons who came to the south and spread toward the north.

None of these new peoples had ever been Roman subjects. Wherever they settled and took control, Roman life died out. We do not know what happened to the Christian religion in England. The Celts probably kept their beliefs but lost their organized church. Christianity was brought back again in 597.

The last successful invasion, depicted at right, was in 1066. After the Battle of Hastings, William of Normandy proclaimed himself king of England.

Olmiodum vero Idem
Gullermus dur in die natalis domini ab Aerlando

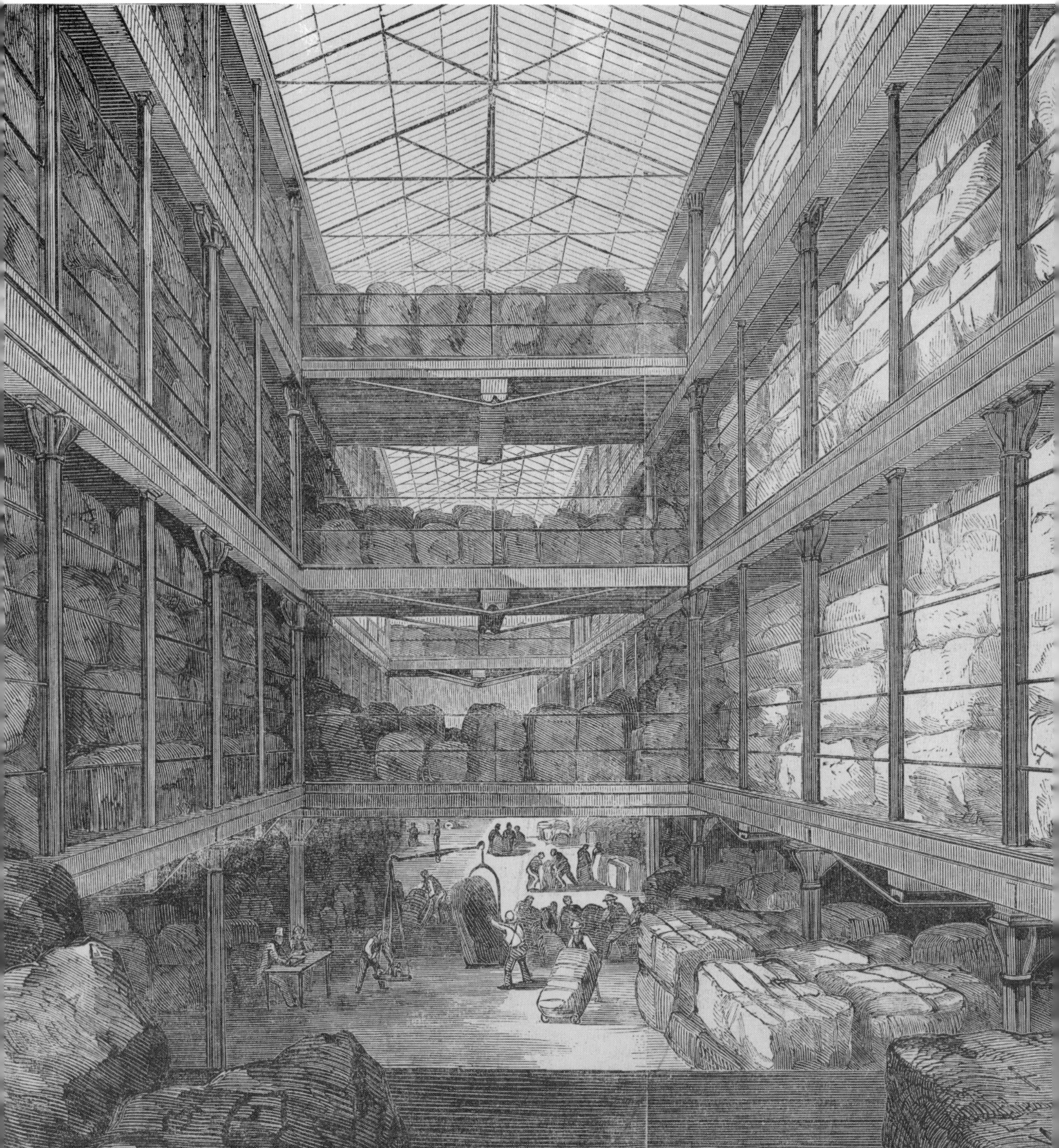

In time the invaders came to control most of England, although Cornwall and Cumbria remained Celtic for a long time.

After 800 pirates from Denmark and Norway, called Vikings, began to raid the coasts of the British Isles. Then they began to settle in places they had raided. Viking villages grew up around the coasts of Ireland and Scotland and in southwest Wales and the Isle of Man. It was mainly Vikings from Denmark who came to England. They conquered the north and east. In 1013 England had a Danish king and was for a time part of the Danish empire.

By 1065, before the last invasion, the people of Great Britain were already mixed. England had Celts, Saxons, Angles, Jutes, and Vikings. Wales had Celts and some Viking settlements. Scotland had Picts, other Celts, Angles, and Vikings.

The last invaders were Normans. These people came from Normandy in northern France. Their ancestors had been Vikings who had settled there. Their duke, William, conquered England in 1066.

Normans spoke a variety of French that became the important language in the land, except in the Roman Catholic Church, which used Latin. As the English language developed, it included many French and Latin words as well as Celtic and Saxon words. The Norman kings gave England a link with France that lasted for about 400 years.

Scotland had a link with France, too, especially southeastern Scotland. There were also strong links with Norman England. The language spoken in southern Scotland was a mixture of northern English, Norse, the Viking language, and Norman French. The Celts, who lived in clans in the west and north, spoke Gaelic, a Celtic language.

Welsh is also a Celtic language. The kings of England conquered Wales in 1282. At first this did not have much effect on the language. But by the sixteenth century they also began to make Wales more English. They brought in the English language and Anglican, or English, Christianity.

Then the Protestant religion came to Great Britain, causing civil wars for the next hundred years. Disputes over religion were tangled up with arguments about national freedom and self-government.

In 1603 the king of Scotland, James VI, became James I of England as well. But the two countries did not share a government until 1707. The kings of England had partly ruled Ireland since the twelfth century. They had control of all Ireland by 1600 and continued to maintain control until 1921. Then the northeast corner chose to remain under English rule.

After 1760 two big changes produced more mixing of nationalities. New industries were developing, and people moved around the country looking for work in factory towns. There was new interest in countries overseas, and people from all parts of the British Isles left home to found colonies abroad. The colonies later became a Commonwealth.

In the twentieth century this Commonwealth sent many people to live in Britain. Most of them came from India, Pakistan, and the West Indies.

By the early nineteenth century England was the world's center of trade and commerce. Here is a view of the great wool floor at the London docks.

These are two knights of the order of St. John of Jerusalem. In 1530 Malta became their headquarters.

MALTA

Malta is a group of five islands that lie south of Sicily in the Mediterranean sea. Gozo, Comino, and the biggest island, also called Malta, are inhabited. No one lives on the islands of Comminotto and Filfla because they are so tiny.

People have lived in Malta since at least 3800 BC. The Carthaginians from north Africa were there from about 600 BC, but they lost Malta to the Romans in 218 BC.

As a part of the Roman Empire, Malta became Christian. The people are thought to have been converted by St. Paul.

After AD 395 Malta was supposed to be part of the eastern half of the Roman Empire. In fact the Arabs from north Africa and the Middle East had more effect on life and ideas in Malta than the eastern empire did. After the year 1000 there was frequent contact with Sicily. The Maltese language grew as a mixture of Sicilian and Arabic.

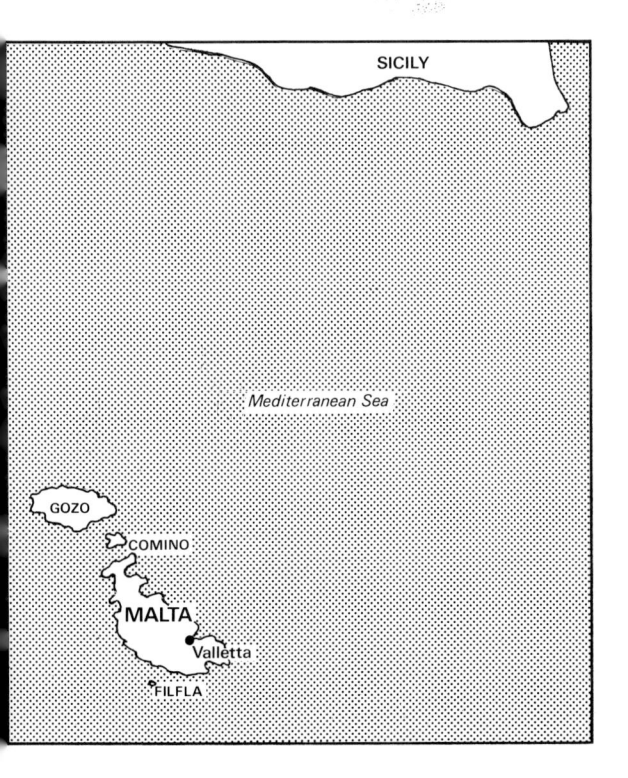

During the Middle Ages European knights formed a company, or order, to protect Christian pilgrims visiting Jerusalem. They were called the order of the Knights Hospitaler of St. John of Jerusalem. In 1530 Malta became their main base in the Mediterranean. Valletta, the capital, was their fortress. It was named after their Grand Master, Jean de la Valette. Malta was attacked more than once by the knights' enemies. Maltese people outside Valletta tended to live in groups of villages that could be easily defended.

In 1798 Malta was conquered by the French. In 1802 it was given back to the knights. The Maltese protested this. The knights left, and Malta became a British colony in 1814.

Malta was still an ideal base for a navy in the Mediterranean. It became a military base for the British as it had been for the knights. By the end of World War II in 1945, the Maltese wanted to control their own future and be something more than a fortress. Malta became an independent country in 1964. The British base closed in 1979.

MONACO

Monaco is a very small country called a "principality," set into the Mediterranean coast of France, near Nice. The people speak French and Monegasque, a mixture of French and Italian. Since 1297 they have been ruled by the Grimaldi family, Princes of Monaco. (See map on page 20.)

DENMARK

Denmark is a flat country almost surrounded by sea, made up of a peninsula and a group of islands. No place in Denmark is far from the North Sea or the Baltic Sea.

The people of Denmark are Scandinavians, like their neighbors the Norwegians and the Swedes. All Scandinavian people began with the same language, and the same customs, and worshipped the same gods: Woden, Thor, and Freyr. They admired a good fighter and were impressed by wealth.

After about AD 750 some of these people, known as Vikings, became pirates and sea raiders. Danish Vikings raided England, France, and North Germany and were greatly feared.

After AD 900 there was a slow change. The Danes were becoming Christian and were also forming themselves into a separate country, with a king. Even the Vikings turned to trade instead of looting. Many left Denmark and settled down in the lands they had raided.

The Danes who stayed home mainly farmed, fished, and sailed. Denmark had a navy and an important merchant fleet. Much of Danish history is about Danes, Swedes, and North Germans competing for control of the all-important Baltic Sea. At first the Danes held southern Sweden and controlled both sides of the entrance to the Baltic. In 1537 they took over Norway and the distant Norwegian settlements in the Faeroe Islands and Iceland.

In 1660 the Swedes drove the Danes out of south Sweden, so the Danes lost their best farmland and their hold on the Baltic

The area of Schleswig-Holstein was disputed between Denmark and Germany for centuries. Here, Danish artillery and infantry are in action in 1850.

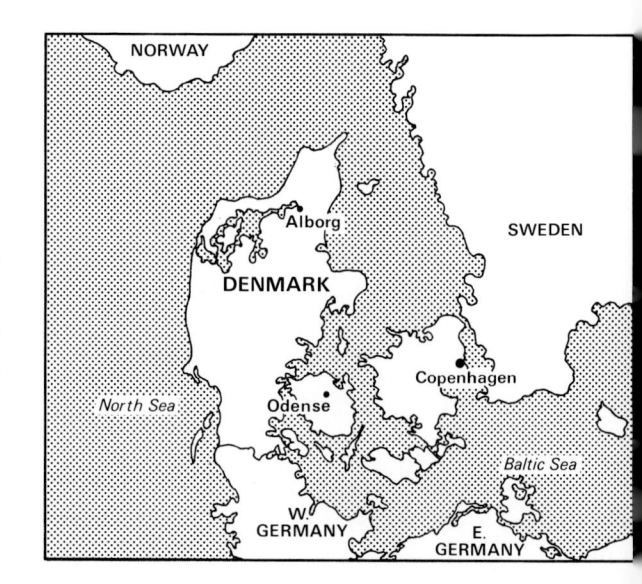

Sea. They still had trade in the north Atlantic, with Iceland and the Faeroe Islands. In 1721 they went even farther northwest and founded a colony in Greenland in North America. In 1814 they had to give up Norway, but they kept the Faeroe Islands and Iceland.

Denmark has one land frontier, the German frontier to the south. German families have moved into Denmark from earliest times and so have German ideas. Denmark was one of the first countries to adopt the teaching of Martin Luther, the German religious reformer, in the sixteenth century. But there have been wars in Denmark, too. The southern frontier has been moved more than once. On either side of it there are still areas of mixed population. Some Danish descendants live in what is now Germany, and some German descendants live in what is now Denmark.

Denmark is still a kingdom, and Greenland and the Faeroe Islands are still part of it. Iceland is an independent country.

ISLE OF MAN

The Isle of Man is a part of the British Isles and is situated in the Irish Sea. It belongs to the British Crown. The people, of Celtic and Viking descent, are called Manx. (See map on page 44.)

CHANNEL ISLANDS

The Channel Islands — Jersey, Guernsey, Alderney, Sark, and others — are in the English Channel and belong to the British Crown. The people are of French and English descent. (See map on page 20.)

Jersey, in the Channel Islands, was the site of the last French invasion against Britain. This famous painting depicts an episode in the Battle of Jersey in 1781.

HUNGARY

The size of Hungary has changed many times. It has been a small place in the west of the present country, It has also been big enough to embrace the eastern part of Czechoslovakia, the western part of Romania, and a large area in Yugoslavia.

Originally there were tribes of farmers living on the plain by the Danube River, which flows down through the middle of modern Hungary. The Romans invaded the land west of the Danube, but their empire broke up during the fourth century.

Tribes from Germany and the east came swarming in. The land was flat and lay around a river deep enough for large boats, so movements of thousands of people were fairly easy.

The Magyar people arrived from Russia at the end of the ninth century AD. They were herders and fierce raiders. Each tribe had its chief, and the tribes were organized in clans or families. The tribes lost their power as the Magyars settled down, but clans were important for a long time.

The Magyars settled in Transylvania, which is now in Romania, in 896. From there they spread into Hungary. They raided the people around them and were greatly feared. When they raided Germany, however, they were defeated. That was in 955, and afterwards the Magyar leaders thought it wiser to make friends with the Germans. They were converted to the Germans' Roman Catholic faith. On Christmas Day in the year 1000 their chief, Stephen I, was crowned as Christian king of Hungary.

During the next hundred years Slovakia, Transylvania, and Croatia came under Hungarian rule. These places are now in Czechoslovakia, Romania, and Yugoslavia. The king ruled the country through his nobles, or magnates, who helped him to defend it. The main threat was from the southeast, where the Turks, Muslims from Asia, had invaded Europe.

The Turks conquered most of Hungary in 1526. The only part they did not control was the western end. This was ruled by Ferdinand of Hapsburg, who claimed the Hungarian throne. He was also ruler of one of the many German-speaking states, Austria. In 1558 he became overlord of all the German states as well.

Ferdinand turned his part of Hungary into a line of fortresses to keep the Turks away. In 1699 the Turks were defeated altogether. By that time the Hapsburg family had an empire which included Austria and Hungary. It was ruled from the Austrian capital city, Vienna. The Austrians were the most influential people in the Hapsburg empire.

The Magyar leaders had to learn the Austrians' German language and Austrian ways of doing things. During the next 200 years they succeeded so well that their own Magyar language went out of fashion. Then, in the nineteenth century, some Hungarians tried to revive their national language and national identity because they felt that the Austrians were replacing both.

The trouble was that not all Hungarians were Magyars. There were Slovaks in Slovakia, Romanians in Transylvania, and Croats in Croatia. There were many descendants of German or Austrian soldiers and settlers, and there were refugees from the Turkish empire. All these people had their own languages and did not want Magyar forced upon them. They felt about the Magyars in the same way the Magyars felt about the Austrians.

In 1918 the Austrians were defeated in World War I, and their empire broke up. Hungarian magnates hoped to be able to keep their own big kingdom, but the lands of the Slovaks, Romanians, and Croats were given to new countries. Those lands also had many Magyars, who were cut off from Hungary.

The new, small Hungary became a communist state in 1946, which it remains.

PORTUGAL

Portugal is a small country with a long coastline beside the Atlantic Ocean. The climate is damp and temperate. Only the northeast has a harsher climate, like the neighboring part of Spain.

You might want to read about Spain first, because Portugal was part of Spain until 1139. At that time it belonged to the kingdom of Castile, in central Spain.

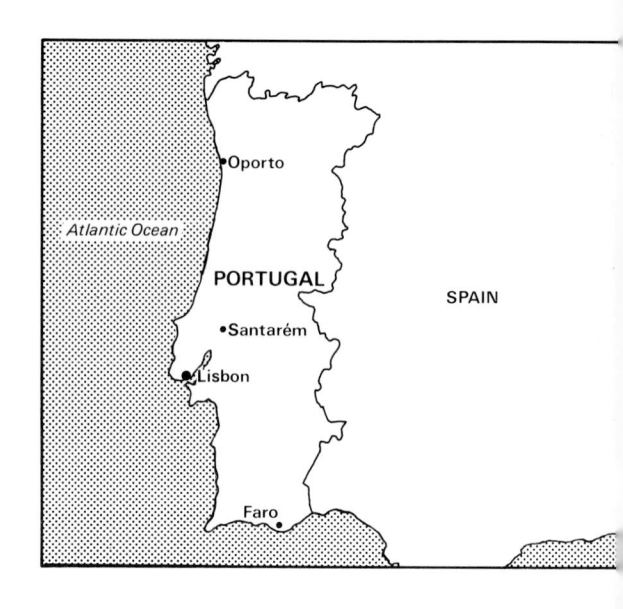

The king of Castile was fighting the Muslim rulers of southern Spain. His cousin, Henry of Burgundy, came to help. Henry was put in charge of Portugal. His son took the title of king in 1139 and ruled over northern and central Portugal. The rest was gradually won from the Moors.

The Portuguese won more land overseas. From their long coast and many ports they sailed out to take new colonies. During the fifteenth century, in light, sturdy ships called caravels, they traveled far around the coast of Africa and out to Atlantic islands. After 1500 they founded colonies in the Far East and in South America. The largest of these was Brazil.

Portuguese settlers took with them Roman Catholicism and their skills in farming, mining, and forestry. From their colonies great wealth came back to Portugal. The country became a market for goods from all over the world.

During the nineteenth century the royal family, the Braganças, became unpopular and there were uprisings against them. Portugal became a republic after a 1910 revolution. By that time much of the overseas trade had gone elsewhere. Most of the empire had become independent by 1980.

This is Prince Henry the Navigator. The voyages of exploration he encouraged in the fifteenth century led to the discovery of the sea route to India and to the vast Portuguese empire.

AUSTRIA

The early people of Austria were Celtic. The Romans conquered them about 58 BC. The Romans built many forts along the Danube River, which was their frontier.

The Roman empire ended during the fifth century AD, but Austria was still a frontier state. German tribes invaded Austria and tried to hold it against enemies from the east, Slavs from Bohemia, and Magyars from Hungary.

In AD 1282 the German king, Rudolf of Hapsburg, made his sons rulers of Austria. The Slav and Magyar rulers never conquered the land again, but some Slav and Magyar settlers went on living there under the new German dukes.

The Hapsburg family became extremely powerful. In 1438 they were the hereditary kings of Germany, heads of all the small German states. One branch of the family went on to rule Spain and part of Italy. The other branch stayed in Austria and transformed it into an important country, with an enormous empire in southeastern Europe.

This empire was founded in 1526. When the king of the neighboring countries of Hungary and Bohemia was killed in battle, Ferdinand of Hapsburg, ruler of Austria, was chosen to succeed him. The empire lasted until 1918. It reached eastward into Romania, southward into Yugoslavia, and northward into Poland. The people of the empire were Germans, Magyars, and Slavs. People of all these nationalities were living in Vienna, the capital city of Austria. In the Austrian countryside and the small towns, most of the people were German.

There were many problems, as people in the different parts of the empire wanted more freedom. Many Austrians felt that their German neighbors were their natural allies and that Slavs and Magyars were a souce of trouble. German-speaking Austrians were also impressed by the strength and wealth of the newly united Germany.

In 1914 Austria and Germany were allies in World War I. They lost, and one of the results of this was that the empire ended. All the Slav and Magyar states that wanted independence then had it.

In 1938 Germany took over Austria. Germany lost World War II in 1945 and Austria once again became a separate country.

This is Maria Theresa, Queen of Hungary and of Bohemia, and Archduchess of Austria. Her accession caused the War of the Austrian Succession and was later a partial cause of the Seven Years' War.

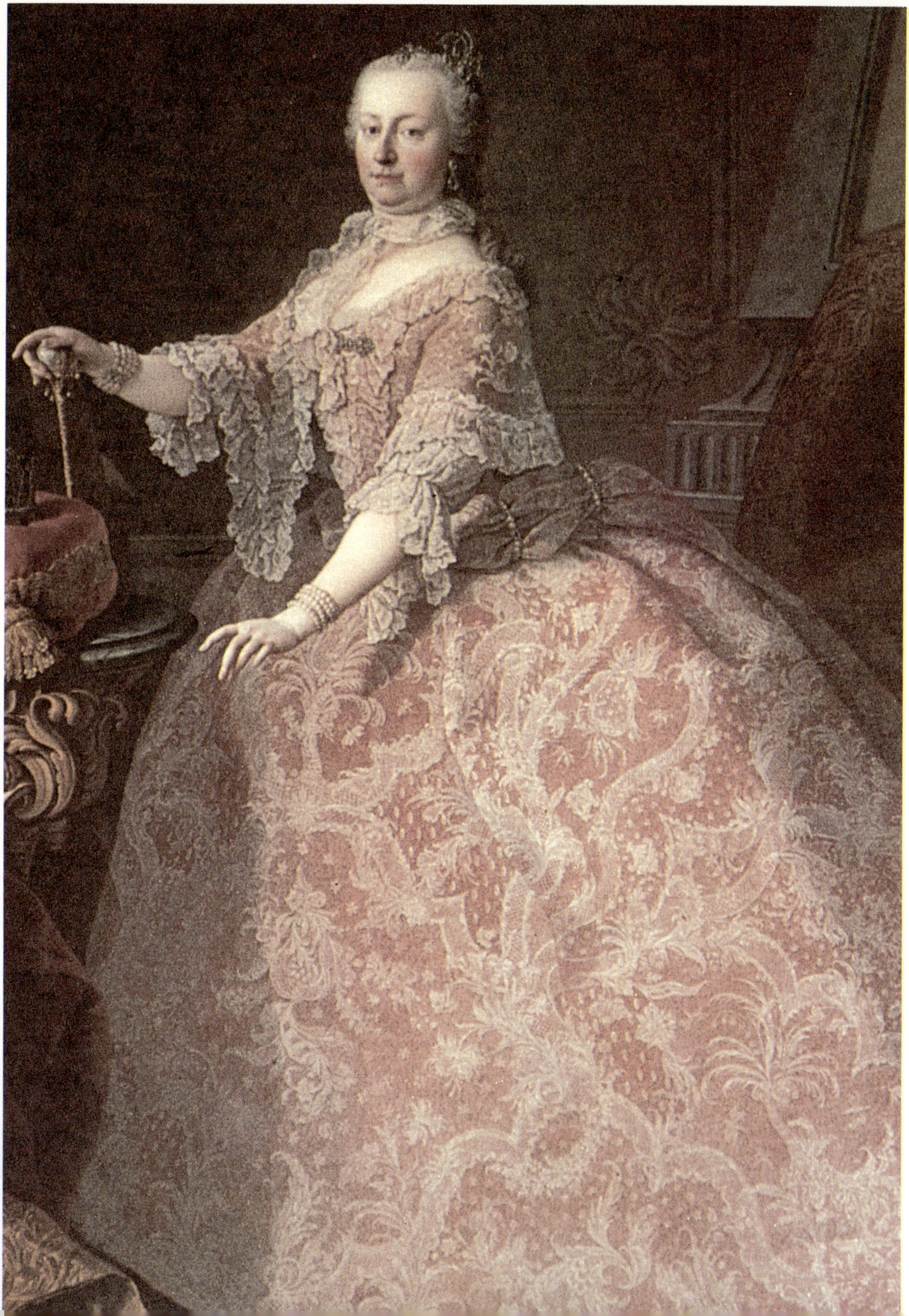

ALBANIA

Albania is a small country with rugged mountains. It has been invaded and divided many times. Various parts of the country have been settled by Greeks, Romans, Bulgarians, Slavs, and Turks, but none of these peoples have ever driven the native Albanians out of the mountains.

The Albanians are probably descended from the Illyrians, who lived in this area from at least 1000 BC. After 620 BC the Greeks founded two colonies in Albania. In time, Greek ideas spread out into the surrounding country, which at that time was divided between many rulers. The king of Illyria was the most important. He fought many wars with his powerful neighbor, the king of Macedonia.

The Illyrians and the Macedonians both held parts of Albania. They in turn were conquered by the Romans. After a battle in 168 BC the land that is now Albania became part of the Roman empire. The Greek cities became even more important under Roman rule. The Roman Empire was divided in AD 395, and Albania was included in the Greek-speaking, or eastern, part.

The eastern emperors were never able to keep out invaders. Tribes from Russia and eastern Europe came into the empire, like the Slavs who attacked Albania. The emperor was unable to defend the Albanian people. The Albanian chieftains had to do it themselves. They built fortified towns and used their own armies. Before long they were the real rulers of the country, but besides fighting the Slavs, they also fought each other.

The Turks, from Asia, were the next invaders. They were not warlike tribes but professional soldiers. To defeat them, the chiefs had to unite, but they could not do it.

The Turks became overlords of Albania after 1390. There were rebellions against them, especially under the soldier George Kastriote Skanderbeg, but the Turks had complete control by 1506. They ruled Albania until 1912. They brought in the Muslim religion, which became the faith of most Albanians.

When Turkish rule ended, the Albanians wanted one independent country for all the people who spoke the Albanian language. They found it hard to convince other countries that they were a nation with a language and a culture of their own.

The Albanians declared themselves independent in 1912. There was still disagreement between different groups and political parties within Albania, as there had been between the medieval chiefs. There were also more invasions, especially during World War I, from 1914-18.

Italy invaded and occupied Albania from 1939 until 1944. After the occupation ended, the country became independent, with a communist government.

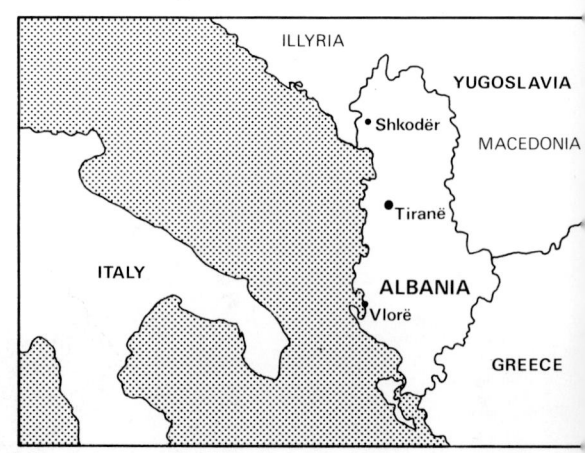

ICELAND

Iceland is a large island in the north Atlantic Ocean. Most of it is made up of mountains, of which many are volcanoes, and vast areas of ice and volcanic lava. Nearly all the towns or villages are near the coast.

The first villages were founded by Vikings, people who came by sea from Norway in about AD 874. Vikings were soldiers, pirates, traders, and explorers. They were practical and fierce. They brought groups of settlers to the island. Some groups of Viking settlers came from Norway and some from Viking colonies in Ireland, Scotland, and the Isle of Man.

For a long time the Icelanders ruled themselves. But in 1264 they agreed to be ruled by Norway. When Norway was taken over by Denmark in 1537, Iceland was too.

Iceland was always a difficult country to live in because the land and the climate made farming very hard. The people depended on the sea for fishing and shipping.

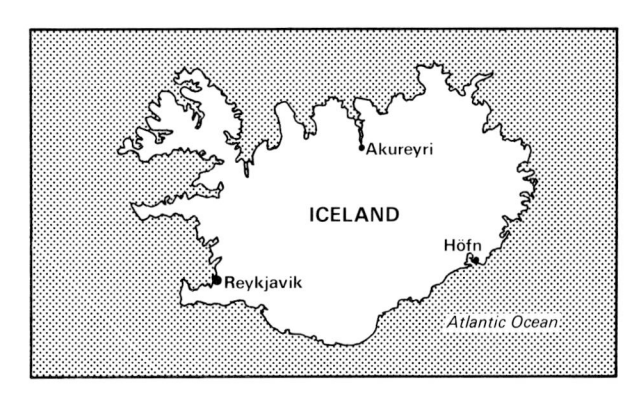

During World War II (1939-45) Iceland was an American military base. This brought the country some prosperity, and in 1944 the Icelanders declared themselves independent of Denmark. Despite their independence, they are still very much like the people of Denmark and Norway in their language and way of life.

Iceland owes its existence entirely to volcanic action. Here is the volcano of Hekla in eruption.

GIBRALTAR

The name "Gibraltar" comes from *Gebel Tarik,* "the Rock of Tarik." Tarik was an African warrior who landed on this rocky peninsula off the southern coast of Spain in AD 711. His followers set up an African Muslim kingdom there. The Spaniards took Gibraltar in 1462. In 1713 Gibraltar became a British colony, which it still is. Most of the people are of Spanish or Portuguese descent. The people speak English and Spanish. Gibraltar is important because it guards the entrance to the Mediterranean Sea. (See map on page 4.)

SAN MARINO

San Marino is a very small republic of only 24 square miles (61 sq km). It lies within the Apennine Mountains in Italy. San Marino has existed since before AD 400. At that time there were many tiny states in Italy with Italian-speaking people. When the states joined the new united kingdom of Italy in 1861-70, San Marino chose to remain independent. (See map on page 12.)

These are two views of Gibraltar. This rocky land at the southern tip of Spain has been a British possession since 1713.

GLOSSARY

Celts: An ancient people of northwestern Europe of whom Irish, Welsh, and Bretons are the main descendants.

Franks: An ancient Germanic people who conquered France about AD 500.

Illyria: An ancient country on the eastern Adriatic coast.

Magyars: A people who originated in the area of modern Hungary.

Middle Ages: The period covering the fifth to fourteenth centuries in Europe.

Muslims: Members of the faith founded in Arabia in the seventh century AD. Early Muslims invaded and settled in southern Spain and most of the Balkans.

Normans: A branch of the Vikings who, in the tenth century AD, conquered Normandy and settled there. In the eleventh century they conquered Britain.

Orthodox Church: A Christian church of the countries in the eastern Roman Empire and a few other countries of eastern Europe.

Protestant Church: A group of Christian churches which separated from the Roman Catholic Church beginning in the sixteenth century.

Roman Catholic Church: A Christian church that accepts the Bishop of Rome, the Pope, as its supreme head.

Roman Empire: The empire established by the Romans in the first century BC. It eventually covered all the countries of the Mediterranean and all of Europe up to the Rhine and Danube. At the end of the fourth century AD, it was divided into Western and Eastern Empires. The Western Empire ended in AD 476. The Eastern Empire, ruled from Byzantium, renamed Constantinople and now called Istanbul, lasted until the fifteenth century.

Romans: The people of the Roman Empire, its armies, and its settlers.

Slavs: A race of peoples widely spread over eastern, southern, and central Europe — including Russians, Bulgars, Serbs, Croats, Slovenes, Poles, Czechs, Moravians, and Slovaks.

Thrace: An ancient region in the Balkan Peninsula roughly corresponding to modern Bulgaria, Greece, and European Turkey.

Turks: Muslim invaders from Turkey who colonized the Balkans and Greece between the fifteenth and early twentieth centuries.

Vikings: Scandinavian sea raiders, and later settlers, around and on the coasts of northwestern Europe between the eighth and tenth centuries AD.

World War I (1914-18): During this war, the Allies, including the United States and Canada, fought against the Germans in Europe and the Middle East. At its conclusion, various German territories in the Far East and Pacific were handed over to one or the other of the victorious powers.

World War II (1939-45): During this war, the Allies fought against the Japanese in the Far East and the Pacific. At its conclusion, Japan lost its overseas possessions.

INDEX

A

Africa/Africans 4, 54
Albania (Albanians) 24, 25, 38, 58
Andorra (Andorrans) 26
Asia/Asians 12, 25, 26, 29, 32, 40, 53
Asturias 4
Austria (Austrians) 7, 14, 18, 23, 24, 25, 31, 32, 37, 42, 53, 54, 56
Azores (Azoreans) 11

B

BATTLES
　　Battle of Hastings 45; Battle of Jersey 52; Battle of Lutzen 27
Bavaria (Bavarians) 30, 36
Belgium (Belgians) 6-7, 8, 15, 23
Bohemia 36, 37, 56
Braila 35
Brandenburg Gate 30
Britain (British) 10, 12, 13, 33, 34, 47, 49, 51, 52, 60, 61 (see also United Kingdom)
Bruges 6, 7
Bulgaria (Bulgarians) 25, 28-30, 38, 58
Byzantium 24, 29, 38

C

Carthage (Carthaginians) 4, 49
Channel Islands (Channel Islanders) 52
Constantinople 24, 38
Cumbria 47
Cyprus (Cypriots) 32-33
Czechoslovakia (Czechoslovakians) 32, 36-37, 53, 54 (see also Slovakia)

D

Dalmatia 24, 25
Democratic Republic, German (East Germany) 32
Denmark (Danes) 10, 19, 20, 26, 28, 34, 44, 47, 50-51, 59
Dodona 41
Dutch (see Holland)

E

East Germany (East Germans) 30
EMPIRES
　　Austrian 18, 23, 24, 37; Austro-Hungarian 25; Bulgar 29; Cretan 38; Frankish 6, 7, 20, 23, 30, 31; German 24; Great Moravian 36; Greek 38, 40, 58; Holy Roman 31, 32; Macedonian 28; Portuguese 55; Roman 4, 6, 12, 13, 15, 20, 23, 24, 28, 32, 33, 34, 36, 38, 42, 44, 49, 53, 56; Slavic 18; Spanish 5; Turkish 29, 30, 35
England (English) 11, 21, 44, 46, 50 (see also United Kingdom)
Europe/Europeans 4, 5, 12, 15, 58

F

Faeroe Islands (Faeroe Islanders) 19, 34, 50, 51
Federal Republic of Germany (West Germany) 32
Finland (Finns) 8-9, 26, 27, 28
Flanders 6, 7
France (French) 4, 5, 7, 8, 14, 16, 20, 21-23, 26, 30, 32, 42, 44, 47, 49, 50, 52

G

Germany (Germans) 7, 9, 13, 15, 16, 17, 18, 19, 20, 23, 27, 28, 30-32, 34, 35, 36, 37, 42, 44, 50, 51, 53, 54, 56
Gibraltar (Gibraltarians) 60
Great Britain (British) (see England and United Kingdom)
Great Moravia 36
Greece (Greeks) 4, 12, 14, 24, 25, 32, 33, 38-40, 58
Greenland 51

H

Hercegovina 25
Holland (Dutch) 7, 8, 14, 15-16, 23
Hungary (Hungarians) 24, 25, 35, 36, 53-54, 56
Hussites 36, 37

I

Iceland (Icelanders) 19, 20, 50, 51, 59
India 47
Ireland (Irish) 10-11, 44, 47 (see also United Kingdom)
Irish Free State 11
ISLANDS
　　Aegean 40; Alderney 52; Atlantic 54; Azores 11, 55; Balearic Islands 6; Channel Islands 52; Comino 49; Comminotto 49; Corsica 23; Crete 38; East Indies 14, 16; Faeroe Islands 19, 34, 50, 51; Filfla 49; Gotland 26, 27; Gozo 49; Guernsey 52; Ibiza 6; Ionian Islands 38; Jersey 52; Macao 55; Madiera 55; Majorca 6; Minorca 6; Öland 26, 27; Sardinia 12; Sark 52; Sicily 12, 14, 49; Siphnos 41; Spitsbergen 20; West Indies 16, 47
Isle of Man (Manx) 47, 51
Istanbul 24, 29, 38
Italy (Italians) 12-14, 38, 42, 60

K

Kingdom of the Serbs, Croats, and Slovenes 25
KINGDOMS
　　Anjou 21; Aquitaine 21; Aragon 5; Brittany 21; Burgundy 20; Castile 4, 5, 54; Connaught 10; Granada 5; Leinster 10; Magyar 34; Munster 10; Navarre 5; Normandy 20; Piedmont-Sardinia 14; Provence 20; Savoy 42; Ulster 10 Knights of St. John of Jerusalem 48, 49

L

LANGUAGES
　　Albanian 58; Arabic 49; Basque 4; Bulgarian 29; Catalan 26; Celtic 47; Czech 36, 37; Dutch 6, 8, 15; English 11, 47, 60; Etruscans 12; Finnish 9; French 6, 8, 23, 26, 42, 47, 49; Gaelic 47; Gallic 20; German 9, 18, 23, 24, 31, 37, 42, 53, 56; Germanic 15, 30; Greek 24, 28, 29, 32, 38, 40; Italian 42; Latin 12, 24, 34; Letzeburgesch 23; Magyar 54; Maltese 49; Monegasque 49; Norman French 47; Norse 47; Provençal 20; Romanian 34; Romansch 42; Russian 18; Scandinavian 50; Serbo-Croatian 24; Sicilian 49; Slavic 29; Spanish 26, 60; Swedish 8, 9; Welsh 47
LEADERS
　　Alexander the Great 38; Barnabas, St. 32; Braganças family 54-55; Calvin, John 15, 35; Cavour, Camillo Benso di 14; Charlemagne 30, 32; Charles of Anjou 21; Constantine 13; Cyril, St. 24; Dermot, King of Leinster 10; Ferdinand of Hapsburg 37, 53, 56; Franco, General Francisco 5; George the Crowned, St. 28; Gregory I, Pope13; Grimaldi princes 49; Gustavus Adolphus 27, 28; Hapsburg emperors 7, 8, 15, 37, 42; Hapsburg princes 56; Hartmann III, Count 9; Henry of Burgundy 54; Henry the Navigator, Prince 55; Huss, Jan 36, 37; Jagiello 18; James I, King 47; James II, King 11; James VI, King (James I) 47; Luther, Martin 27, 31, 35, 51; Marco Polo 12; Maria Theresa 57; Mieszko 18; Napoleon 18, 23, 60; Olaf, St. 20; Olof Skötkonung 27; Otto I, Holy Roman Emperor 31; Paul, St. 32, 49; Philip II, King 28, 38; Popes 14, 18; Rudolf of Hapsburg 56; Skanderbeg, George Kastriote 58; Stephen I, King 53; Tarik 60; Valette, Jean de la 49; William the Conqueror 45, 47; William III 11
Lebanon 4
Liechtenstein (Liechtensteinians) 9
Lithuania 18
Low Countries 7
Luxembourg (Luxembourgians) 23

M

Macedonia (Macedonians) 24, 25, 29-30, 38, 40, 58
Malta (Maltese) 48-49
Moldavia 34, 35
Monaco (Monegasques) 49
Moravia 36, 37
MOUNTAINS
　　Alps 12; Apennines 12, 60; Ardennes 23; Pindus 38; Pyrenees 4, 26

63

N

Netherlands (*see* Holland)
North America 51
Northern Ireland (*see* United Kingdom)
Norway (Norwegians) 10, 19-20, 26, 28, 34, 47, 50, 59

O

OCEANS
Arctic 28; Atlantic 4, 19, 54, 55, 59

P

Pakistan 47
PEOPLES
Alemanni 30; Angles 44, 47; Arabs 49; Basques 4, 6; Belgae 6; Bulgars 29; Burgundians 20, 42; Celts 4, 6, 10, 11, 20, 23, 42, 44, 47, 51, 56; Croats 24-25; Dorians 38; Etruscans 12; Flemish 8; Franks 6, 7, 15, 20, 23, 30; Frisians 15, 30; Gauls 20; Germanic 30, 36, 42, 53, 56; Goths 13; Illyrians 24, 38, 58; Jutes 44, 47; Lapps 8, 9, 19; Latins 12; Lombards 13; Lusitanians 4; Magyars 31, 34, 35, 36, 37, 53, 54, 56; Manx 51; Masovians 17; Mongols 18; Moors 4, 5, 54; Moriscos 4; Moszarabs 4; Mudejars 4; Normans 14, 47; Picts 44, 47; Polians 17; Samnites 12; Saxons 30, 44, 47; Scandinavians 19, 28, 50; Serbians 24, 25; Silesians 17; Slavs 17, 24, 25, 29, 31, 36, 37, 38, 56, 58; Svear 26, 27; Tartars 18; Thracians 24, 28, 34, 38; Thuringians 30; Vikings 6, 10, 19, 20, 26, 34, 47, 50, 51, 59; Vlachs 38; Walloons 8

PLAINS
Danube 34; Latium 12

Poland (Poles) 17, 19, 32, 36, 56
Portugal (Portuguese) 4, 11, 54-55, 60
Prussia (Prussians) 18, 31, 32

R

RELIGIONS
Bogomil 24, 25; Celtic tribal 11; Christianity 6, 10, 11, 12, 13, 15, 18, 20, 24, 27, 29, 31, 32, 34, 36, 38, 40, 42, 44, 49, 50; Eastern Orthodoxy 28, 34, 36, 38; Greek Orthodoxy 24, 25, 29, 32, 40; Islam 4, 25, 29, 34, 53, 54, 58, 60; Lutheranism 31; Muslim (*see* RELIGIONS:Islam); non-Christian 18;

Norse 50; Protestantism 11, 15, 20, 22, 27, 34, 35, 42, 47, 51; Roman Catholicism 4, 5, 6, 8, 11, 13, 15, 17, 18, 20, 21, 22, 23, 24, 25, 31, 34, 35, 36, 38, 42, 53, 54; Viking 27

Republic of Ireland (*see* Ireland)
REVOLUTIONS
French 22-23; Russian 9
RIVERS
Danube 12, 28, 34, 53, 56; Maritsa 28; Po 12; Rhine 6, 12, 15, 30, 42; Scheldt 6, 8; Tyne 44; Volga 8

Romania (Romanians) 34-35, 38, 53, 54, 56
Rome (Romans) 4, 6, 12, 13, 14, 18, 20, 21, 24, 26, 33, 34, 38, 42, 44, 49, 53, 56
Russia (Russians) 8, 9, 18, 19, 26, 28, 30, 32, 35, 36, 53, 58

S

St. John of Jerusalem, Knights of 48, 49
San Marino (San Marinese) 14, 60
Schleswig-Holstein 50, 51
Scotland (Scots) 11, 44, 47 (*see also* United Kingdom)
SEAS
Adriatic 38; Aegean 38, 40; Baltic 8, 18, 26, 27, 50; Black 18, 34; Irish 51; Mediterranean 4, 6, 12, 14, 32, 49, 60; North 26, 50

SETTLEMENT
through colonization
  Iceland 59
through conquest
  Ireland 11; Sweden 28
through farming
  Finland 8; Portugal 54; Sweden 27
through forestry
  Portugal 54
through invasion
  Albania 58; Cyprus 32; England 44, 47; Switzerland 42
through mining
  Portugal (in Brazil) 54; Sweden 27
through trade
  Belgium 6-7; Cyprus 32; Holland 15; Spain 6, 7; Sweden 26

Slovenia (Slovenes) 24, 25
Spain (Spanish) 4-6, 7, 14, 26, 54, 60, 61
Sparta 38
Stockholm 26, 27
Sweden (Swedes) 8, 19, 20, 26-28, 50
Switzerland (Swiss) 42-43

Syria 32

T

Toggenburg 43
Transylvania 34, 35, 53, 54
Tribes (*see* PEOPLES)
Turkey (Turks) 25, 29, 30, 32, 33, 34, 35, 38, 39, 40, 53, 54, 58

U

United Kingdom (British *and* Irish) 10, 11, 44-47 (*see also separate entries for* Britain, England, Ireland, Scotland, *and* Wales)
United States 10, 11, 59

V

Valletta 49
VALLEYS
Po 12; Valley of Roses 29
Vatican City 14
Venice 12, 14, 24
Vienna 53, 56
VOLCANOES
Hekla 59; Santorini 38

W

Walachia 34, 35
Wales (Welsh) 44, 47 (*see also* United Kingdom)
WARS
Battle of the Boyne 11; Hundred Years' War 21; Irish Civil 11; Seven Years' War 57; Spanish Civil War 5-6; Thirty Years' War 27, 28; War of Austrian Succession 57; World War I 8, 9, 32, 54, 56, 58; World War II 9, 19, 30, 31, 35, 37, 49, 56, 59

Y

Yugoslavia (Yugoslavs) 24-25, 38, 40, 53, 54, 56

Picture Acknowledgments— Austrian Institute 57; Author 22, 25, 39, 46, 50-51; Belgian Embassy 6; Bodleian Library 12, 13, 16, 21, 32, 45; Bulgarian Cultural Institute 28, 29; Cedok (London) Ltd. 37; Cyprus High Commission 33; Embassy of Federal Republic of Germany 30, 31; Embassy of Iceland 59; Finnish Tourist Board 9; Gibraltar Government Tourist Office 60, 61; Mary Evans Picture Library 35, 48; National Library of Ireland 10, 11; National Tourist Organization of Greece 41; Patrimonie des Musees Royaux des Beaux-Arts, Brussels 7; Portuguese National Tourist Office 55; Rijksmuseum-Stichting, Amsterdam 14; Royal Netherlands Embassy 15; Royal Norwegian Embassy 21; Societe Jersiase 52; Spanish National Tourist Office 5; Swedish Institute 26, 26-27; Swiss National Tourist Office 43; Young Library 40.